LEZ TALK

A COLLECTION OF BLACK LESBIAN SHORT FICTION

LEZ TALK

A COLLECTION
OF BLACK LESBIAN
SHORT FICTION

EDITED BY S. ANDREA ALLEN & LAUREN CHERELLE

BLF Press
Clayton, NC

Lez Talk: A Collection of Black Lesbian Short Fiction Copyright © 2016 by S. Andrea Allen and Lauren Cherelle. All rights reserved. No part of this publication may be reproduced, distributed, or transmitted in any form or by any means, including photocopying, recording, or other electronic or mechanical methods, without the prior written permission of the publisher, except in the case of brief quotations embodied in critical reviews and certain other noncommercial uses permitted by copyright law. For permission requests, write to the publisher, addressed "Attention: Permissions" at the address below.

Printed in the United States of America

First Printing, 2016

Cover design: Lauren Curry

ISBN: 978-0-9972439-9-4
Library of Congress Control Number: 2016903097

BLF Press
PO Box 833
Clayton, NC 27520

www.blfpress.com

Contents

Introduction

A dream, undeterred

Like many Black lesbian readers, I've been looking for myself in books all of my life. I'd come across a few Black lesbian or bi characters in Alice Walker's *The Temple of My Familiar* and *By the Light of My Father's Smile*, and even in April Sinclair's *Coffee Will Make You Black.* There were other writers out there, but I was really introduced to Black lesbian literature writ large in 2009 while in graduate school. During my research I was introduced to Jewelle Gomez, Pat Parker, and Audre Lorde; and lesser known writers Anita Cornwell, Becky Birtha, and Stephanie Byrd. I also found Skyy of the *Choices* series, Laurinda Brown, and Cheril N. Clarke. It angered me that I had never heard of these writers before, and here I was, a 40-year-old Black lesbian who had been out for nearly two decades!

In 2012, I came out of my dissertation proposal defense and remarked to Evie Blackwood that perhaps one day I'd start my own Black lesbian feminist press as a way to pay homage to Barbara and Beverly Smith and their Kitchen Table: Women of Color Press, as well as a way to support and publish Black lesbian writing. For a little while, I put that dream aside and focused on my scholarly work and finding a full-time position in academe. But the more I read about Black lesbian literature, the more I felt drawn to contribute to what I can now assert is a Black lesbian literary canon.

I'll admit that part of my desire to contribute to a body of Black lesbian literature is a bit selfish. I wanted to read Black

INTRODUCTION

lesbian fiction that wasn't full of overly wrought sex scenes or lesbian melodrama. Nor was I interested in "urban fiction," which mostly included some combination of violence, sex, money, or drugs. More than anything, though, I believed that Black lesbians have more stories to tell. Relationship and coming out stories are important, but what other aspects of Black lesbian life have we not yet examined? Toni Morrison says, "If there's a book that you want to read, but it hasn't been written yet, then you must write it." Even as I continued to engage in scholarly work, the urge to tell, as well as to support the telling of these stories, pulled at me daily.

In time, I decided to do a podcast on Black lesbian literature as a way of just reminding folks that Black lesbian writing was out there, and this is how I met Lauren. That Lauren and I met was pure serendipity. Around two years ago, I asked my Sister Outsider blog readers whether they'd be interested in a podcast on Black lesbian literature. I didn't get much of a response, so I set the idea to the side and turned my attention to other things. A few weeks later, I was going through my Gmail junk folder and stumbled upon an email from Lauren who had written that she was not only interested in listening to a podcast, but that she was interested in collaborating on one. We set up a time to talk on the phone, and our partnership was born: two Black lesbian writers, Lauren already a seasoned publisher, and me, a doctoral student with a keen desire to put theory into practice.

I wanted to do more than just read and write *about* Black lesbian literature, I had my own stories to tell. I'd been writing prose my entire life, but I'd always been leery of publishing any of it. Graduate school, however, made me fearless, and I was ready to not only focus on my own writing, but also to create a space for other Black lesbian writers to share their work. I wanted to put together an anthology of Black lesbian short fiction, but I knew that I was long on desire and short on expertise. After getting to know Lauren through our collaboration on our radio show, Lez Talk Books Radio, I asked her if she wanted to partner with me on the anthology. She said yes, and our editorial partnership was born.

Lez Talk: A Collection of Black Lesbian Fiction is a labor of love. We say in our call for submissions: "We operate under the assumption that lesbian is not a dirty word." At a time where a disavowal of any type of stable identity is at an all time high, it is important for us to focus on writing that celebrates Black lesbian identities and amplifies the diversity of Black lesbian experiences.

~*Stephanie*

Writing is not new to us

When considering the lack of control and struggles we endure because of oppressive systems that exploit and repress our Black and lesbian identities, I am not surprised at the proliferation of Black lesbian stories over the past few years. First, a shift in society has allowed more Black lesbian writers to be visible and confident, stretching our narratives and highlighting our identities. Second, thanks to robust digital printing, on-demand publishing, more self-publishing vendors, and advances in e-book technology, our stories are no longer authored by a handful of women.

With that said, I can't neglect the fact that writers had stories to tell and readers to share pieces of our world with *prior* to the current publishing revolution. I realize that, until recently, we didn't have access. Desktop access. Affordable access. Non-discriminatory access. With access, the Black lesbian genre does not have to remain in the belly of underground publishing.

Increased access, however, isn't the bottom line. I believe that publishing (not just writing) has afforded many of us with a modicum of freedom. There is a space in the new publishing playground akin to Lady Justice: blind and objective. Publishing is one of a few avenues where Black lesbians can actually speak things into existence. *This* freedom, a freedom to create and exist without boundaries literally lies at our fingertips.

But, with freedom to create comes a commitment to responsible practices. We should value self and other Black lesbian women enough to create stories that extend cultural representations and incorporate a range of literary devices; stories of responsible quality from writers (and publishers) who edit with care; stories from women who write with purpose. Responsible writers realize that Black lesbian stories are spokes of a collective body; that our stories can bridge geographic and socioeconomic barriers; that our stories are meaningful enough to mitigate social isolation.

Regardless of whether the mainstream publishing arena ever recognizes Black lesbian contributions with integrity and resources, it is our responsibility as readers and writers to continually claim our existence, disseminate our stories, and narrate our journeys.

Hence the beauty of an anthology, which is a vessel that collects our voices, a time capsule that seals writers' imaginations and reflects our hearts' desires. Our desire for *Lez Talk* is to help transform budding writer's '*I've always wanted to*' into '*I will*' statements. We want our efforts to inspire more Black lesbian writers to create critically sound, culturally reflective, and creatively entertaining stories that tap into the intersectionality and complexities of Black womanhood and sexuality. As Barbara Smith pleaded over thirty years ago, we need you to "write about and manifest our lives in every possible way." In other words, we are nowhere near the end of our road.

I am honored to share this road with Stephanie, to celebrate the art of good storytelling and the capacity to extend access to more writers. I champion the responsibility to write and publish as Black + lesbian, and the opportunity to collaborate and foster conversations and community. It saddens me to know that without technology and the Internet, improved access, or a flatter Earth, our corner of the world will remain dim; that the infrastructure that allowed my path to cross with Stephanie's would still be floating in someone's head; that my desire to create and share would be limited to very few places. So, this anthology is part of an advancing beginning, a spoke to connect our journeys and shine light on Black and lesbian, an occasion to give my identities the praise and recognition they both deserve.

~*Lauren*

I Can't Turn It Off
Sheree L. Greer

I watch Akua sleep sometimes. Creepy, I know. But I don't care.
I smile at the slight flare of her nostrils, the delicate puff of air
when she snores. She smells like black soap and cocoa butter. I
imagine us old; black don't crack, so we won't crumble. And at
sixty, Akua's afro is speckled with copper, a contrast to my platinum dreads. We still go for walks, still cuddle to watch movies,
still randomly burst into 90's R&B jams. I smile at the thought,
looking down at her. The sheet pushed down to her waist. Her
skin, warm and brown and catching the blue moonlight through
the blinds just right. I make believe she's been sleeping beside
me forever, and I'm still not tired of it. I love her, and I would
marry her. After all, it's legal now.

Just like killing black kids is.

I didn't mean to mention that.

Don't write angry. Don't drive angry. Don't fuck angry.

I can't help it though.

I kiss Akua awake and look in her eyes as they flutter open.
I kiss her again, a smash of lips, even a grazing of teeth. A bite.
An urgent tongue. I feel heat, from inside. Desire and rage, they

tango, off-beat though. There's a thumping like someone's trapped and trying to get out. We find each other's blaze and we dig it. Sweat runs down my back like oil down a neighborhood street. Yes. Oil down a neighborhood street. That shit really happened. We getting it in now, and it's warm and wet and dark, like a rainy night in Central Florida, like pull up your hood but keep stepping, we're almost home. I'm scared though. Scared of being followed and hunted. But they say they scared of me. I am drowning even though my mouth is dry. I'm thirsty but can't drink the water. These thoughts don't belong, like chemicals I can't pronounce poisoning the river. Wade in the water, children, but it smells funny. Tastes funny. Feels strange against my skin. I'm tingling. Akua reaches up and grabs my face, bringing me back.

"Where are you?" Akua asks.

"I'm here," I say.

She wraps her arms around me, her legs too, tangled in with mine. We connect at all the important parts. Lips, heartbeat, lips. We hold each other closer than close, breathing the same. Akua rolls her body slow, and everything in me clenches with pleasure and fear. My stomach in knots. It aches, feels empty. Like all those folks going hungry since they passed that Farm Bill. They taking stamps, from people who need 'em, from children and families and people who look like my grandparents. And I think I might cry now. From the hunger. I'm starving. I latch my mouth to Akua's breast, sucking, trying to be fed. She moans. My woman, my love, her body curving underneath mine, trying to give me what I need.

Can I trust her? Is she real? Organic?

Maltodextrin. Monosodium glutamate. Cellulose and sodium nitrate. Naked ain't really naked, and we are what we eat. Most nights, I feast on an intelligent Black woman, so I should be all right. Right? I want to ask Akua if she's real, if I can trust her to feed and be fed. If we can live together and keep each other alive.

She's so good to me. Makes sure I get rest and lets me talk shit when I need to, tells me I'm full of shit when she needs to, and maybe this will work. I kiss her again, wanting to feel certain. Let her tongue confess as we touch and agree. Her tongue in my mouth. Her hands on my hips. My mind a frenzy. My heart in my throat. I can't speak but I want to say something important.

I settle for something sweet: "Baby, you feel so good."

Akua moans and smiles.

Does she know I'm all over the place? My mind searching for peace, my heart aching for home? How do I do this? Balance alludes me, and I want to ask for help. Is there anybody out there? I wander up to a stranger's house and ask for assistance. Love thy neighbor.

BLAM! A shot in the face.

I squeeze my eyes tight and try to focus. I kiss Akua's neck and shoulders. Her skin hot, salty, sweet. She pulls me close, and with a swift assertiveness that lets me know she wants to take control, Akua rolls us over. She's on top now, my eyes still closed, darkness swirling as I try to silence the screams. Did Rekia even get a chance to scream? Last words rush my brain, pressing against the back of my teeth.

Please don't let me die. What are you following me for? It's not real. Why did you shoot me? I can't breathe. I love you, too. Mom, I'm going to college.

"You shot me. You shot me," I mumble as Akua's lips graze the paunch of my belly. She kisses my navel and moves her body up.

"What you say, baby?" Akua asks, looking into my eyes.

"You got me," I whisper. "You got me. I'm yours."

Akua bends to press her full lips against each of my eyelids. I keep them closed as she kisses the bridge of my nose, the tip, my top lip, the bottom. Her mouth on my mouth. Gently. Lightly. An invitation, but I'm lost in the darkness. Akua's hands feel their way around all my curves and edges. Her fingers are searching, and then they find me. Akua always finds me. She pushes inside, a stretch of fingers trying to reach me. She knows I'm aching. Hurting. Needing. Wanting. Hoping. For more. More her. More love. More justice. More nourishment. More safety. More. More. I can barely see. I'm sweating and crying.

I wish I could turn it off.

We collapse into each other. Even though I came, I want to go. I want to go somewhere I'm not hated on sight, where our children aren't targets, where people who lack can get what they need, where the water is clean and the food is whole. Where we matter. Where our lives matter.

And there I go again.

Akua kisses me. My lips and cheeks and nose and eyes and forehead and neck. I am thankful that sweat and tears are both salty and wet. If she can't tell the difference, I can't be too ashamed. I turn away from her because I don't trust my expression, smile or frown, grimace or grin. We spoon, our bodies a crescent moon. Akua presses her breasts against my back and kisses my shoulder. She whispers that she loves me and that she believes we can change the world. Humming Mavis Staples, she holds me tight until she falls asleep.

I feel her arms go slack, her breathing rhythmic and deep. I'll wait until she starts snoring before I turn around to look at her, to watch her sleep.

I love her, and I would marry her. After all, it's legal now.

Darker the Berry
K.A. Smith

I considered the selection of fresh produce before me. The peaches were fat and fuzzed, and I couldn't resist gently running my open palm over the ripest ones. The assorted pears, red and gold and green, looked interesting, but I'd never really had a taste for them.

Now the cherries, that was what I'd come to the market for. I was in the mood for something both sweet and tart, something I could let play in and fill my mouth with flavor, tease my tongue with its juices. I found them shining and glistening with fresh droplets of water on them, freshly rinsed from the contraption wired above. They looked delicious and already had my mouth forming an "o"of anticipation.

Then *she* walked up and stood beside me.

At first I thought it was the cute checkout girl I often asked to point me in the direction of goat cheese or coconut milk. Grocery store layouts always baffled me for some reason. I knew people who liked to cruise each aisle looking at all the things they *might* need. Not me. I liked to get in and get out with exactly what I came for.

The clerk, Sara, batted her eyes and tugged at her braids when she talked to me, pointing me down aisle four for something or other. I offered smiles of gratitude in exchange for her assistance, sometimes with a wink. She couldn't have been more than twenty-one or twenty-two, but she was nice and pleasant and always had a smile for me.

But it wasn't Sara standing strangely close to me now. A name badge hung from around her neck. Tonda Lyons. I couldn't quite make out where she worked, the colors on the badge unfamiliar to me. But on the bottom was a red stripe that read "Clearance Level 12." *Must be important.*

Tonda was taller than me, 5'10", 5'11" maybe. Beautiful bald head shining under the store lights. She had a presence about her that didn't require words. I pictured her interrogating someone the way only a person with Clearance Level 12 could. Hands on hips, neck cocked to the side, lips pursed in an *I dare you to lie to me* kind of way. The thought made my back tingle.

Her skin was the color of plums. Cool blue-black with purple undertones. Smooth and taut. My tongue itched suddenly, growing fat and swollen in my mouth. *Sweet and tart.* I bet she fit the bill. Now my mouth was watering.

She reached in front of me, back curving over as she fingered a bunch of grapes, oblong green ones, then the fat reddish ones. I couldn't help watching her. The jumper she wore was riddled with starbursts of color on a navy blue fabric. Splotches of fuchsia, yellow, blue, and green stretched lively across her back and hips. A blot of pink spread across her ripe buttock and my mouth fell open with appreciation.

"I like the fat juicy ones," she said to me with a relaxed look of acknowledgment as she retrieved two bunches of grapes and placed them in her hand basket. *So do I,* I thought continuing my lazy intake of her physique. Fleshy thighs stayed my attention.

Her eyes fell to where my hand hovered over the cherries. I still hadn't made my selection.

"They say the darker the berry, the sweeter the juice."

A surprised sound escaped my throat. "Is that right?" I nodded in her direction, a smile growing on my face. I couldn't take my eyes off of her. She'd gotten more than just my attention. Her words had piqued my interest.

"Oh, yes. Dark skinned fruit always has the *sweetest* juice."

She was surely playing with me now, flirting. Likening herself, her skin tone to that of the fruit in front of me. It dawned on me that moments like this—unexpected, sexy, random—were exactly the moments missing from my life.

I plucked a deep, dark cherry from the open carton and plopped it into my mouth, twisting the stem between my fingers. "Mmm," I sighed, making a big show of my enjoyment. *I can play too.* A bit of juice squirted from the sweet Hudson cherry and landed on my chin.

Before I could wipe it away, she was already stepping in closer. "May I?" She stopped short before grabbing my chin. I simply nodded. *Permission granted.* The pad of her thumb swiped the juice off my chin. Her touch was warm and swift, and I thought of her deft fingers gliding over my skin in other ways.

Dark red juice colored her thumb. I wanted to pull her digit into my mouth and suck the juice off, but she beat me to it. Tonda jammed her thumb in her own mouth and sucked. Eyes closed, lips curled in around her thumb. *Ooh!* The look of pleasure on her face made me twitch between my legs. *I wish I could bring you such pleasure.*

"Doesn't get much sweeter than that." Her soft voice interrupted my thoughts. She looked at me with suggestive eyes, challenging me.

"Why don't we test that theory?" I offered, placing two cartons of cherries in my basket. I've never been one to turn down a challenge.

Just as Tonda was about to speak again, Sara came around the corner. "Do you need any help tonight, Nova?" She was smiling bright, arms pressed back behind her, pushing her small breasts up and out against her green apron.

I clucked my tongue and shook my head slowly, drawing my attention from Tonda to look at the girl. "No, I found what I wanted, sweetie."

Sara looked slowly from me to Tonda then back to me. Her smile faded as she turned her body to face Tonda. She still had a job to do. "And you, *ma'am*. Are you finding everything?" Sara's tone shifted when she addressed Tonda. The bright notes in her voice died and her shoulders fell.

"Actually, where are your chocolates, dear? I'm in an indulgent mood tonight." Tonda's eyes flashed hot, reddish brown around the outer iris. She was looking right at me as she spoke.

"This way." Sara looked over her shoulder at me before guiding Tonda to another aisle for chocolates. I hoped she'd grab something extra dark, something bitter to contrast the sweet bite of the fruit. I grabbed a few soft peaches, a plum the same hue as Tonda and a red pear. *Why not?*

Tonda and I arrived at Sara's register at the same time. I stood behind Tonda, watching her place her items on the conveyor belt. I easily sneaked glances at her high ass and hardy thighs. Her arms were delightful to look at too, long and toned. I imagined them wrapped around my shoulders as we came together, our bodies dancing to a sweet rhythm. Her elbow crinkled and stretched as she moved each item from her basket for Sara to scan and I decided I would like to bite her there. *Soon.*

Sara's cheeks flushed more and more with each scanned item. She looked from Tonda to me, then down at the items she rang up, heat climbing from under her black ringer tee until her neck was almost a deeper shade of brown.

"Forty-two seventy-five." Sara stared up at Tonda, waiting for the dark-skinned beauty to pay. Her eyes lingered on Tonda's face for a moment, then traveled down as far as they could see before the bulk of the register blocked the rest of her view. I wondered for a moment if Sara was comparing herself to Tonda. I hoped she wasn't.

Tonda paid for her items and slowly bagged them while I chatted with Sara. She drifted a few feet away, but was clearly waiting for me.

"Thanks," I said as Sara bagged my fruits and double wrapped the bottle of wine I picked up on the way to the register.

"It's my job," she replied, shrugging and avoiding my gaze.

"You do it really well. Always with a beautiful smile." I handed her my debit card and, despite knowing better, I let our fingers brush together. Sara blushed again, swiped my card, and handed it back.

"Thanks." A lighter note lifted her voice and she handed me my receipt.

"Same time next week?" I asked jokingly.

Sara nodded and smiled a crooked half smile.

I walked over to where Tonda stood waiting, my cool, friendly demeanor slipping as I took in the sight of her again. My desire for something sweet burned at the back of my throat. The way she held herself so strongly, with one hip popped, made me wet between my legs. She was a night I wanted to disappear into.

"So, your place or mine?" she asked, her voice huskier than I remembered.

"How close?"

"Not close enough."

"Mine, then." My place was right around the corner and I wanted to see her naked, spilled like ink across my bed.

"I'll follow."

. . .

We broke two laws getting to my place, one of state and one of physics. Tonda stayed behind me as I led her to my apartment. Her heels punctuated our entry to the foyer and the short climb up the stairs. I felt her fingering the nape of my neck, drawing a circular swirl pattern against my skin, making me tingle all over as I keyed the door. She was close—so close I could smell her scent, a mixture of beauty products and warm skin. I stood to the right, directed her inside, and shut the door behind us.

"Nice place," she said, looking around before locking eyes on me.

"Thank you." I took her bag from her and placed it along with mine on the nearest surface. "May I?" I asked after I'd already stepped toward her, my head angled. Since the moment she sucked the cherry juice off of her thumb I'd wanted to taste her lips, claim them as my own, slip my tongue inside her warmth.

Her chest rose and she nodded. I pulled her close by the waist, angled my chin up, and kissed her bottom lip.

Sweet. So sweet.

She tasted like cherry. And like something dark, spontaneous, maybe even a little reckless. I smiled beneath her lips and claimed them again— harder this time, and with careful teeth. I pressed the fullness of my mouth into hers until her throat loosened. She let out a soft whimper. I licked her lips, tracing from corner to corner with the tip of my tongue, then sucked her bottom lip with a gentle pull until she was panting and pulling me closer than close.

Her skin felt like whipped silk, so light and smooth beneath my fingertips, cool. I wanted to touch her all over.

"You're very good at that," she hummed in my ear before swirling her tongue around my lobe.

I thanked her by kissing her again, then grabbed our bags and pulled her toward the kitchen.

Tonda eased by me, leaning a hip on the granite countertop, a curious energy in her eyes as she pointed to the rack of wine glasses behind me.

"Would you like some wine?" I unwrapped the bottle I just bought, along with our other goodies.

"Please," she said, plucking a cherry from the carton. It didn't go in her mouth right away. She played it along her lips, pushing it forward and pulling it back until the skin grew dull and bruised. Then she opened her mouth just enough to let it fall inside, her lips a perfect pucker as her tongue and teeth toyed with the cherry.

I poured two glasses of wine and watched her mouth move up and down, up and down. As she pushed the pit out of her mouth and slowly licked her lips, I gasped quietly.

She laughed and grabbed another cherry. This one was for me. She leaned across the counter, arm outstretched with the dark red bobble hanging from her fingers. "Open wide." She pushed the fruit into my mouth, along with two of her fingers.

"Mmm," I sang, sucking the juice. Her scent filled the cavern of my mouth until I could smell her deep in my nose. She could consume me completely, overpower me, I was sure. I wanted that.

"Enough of this seduction scene. Give me what I came here for."

Tonda bit down on her lip, the fleshy pink underside partially exposed. For a moment she looked affected, like perhaps I wouldn't give her what she wanted. Then she knotted her fingers in my shirt and tugged me toward her. She was taking what she wanted. She was taking *me*.

"Isn't patience a virtue?" I teased, kissing her on the neck. I bit her there, then licked away the sting. She gasped and let her head fall back.

"For some," she panted. "Not for me."

"Doesn't fruit need time to ripen?" Another question, another bite. This time on her shoulder. She pushed into the bite, asking for another. I obliged.

"There's ripe, darling, and then there is waste." She cupped my hands around her breasts and squeezed.

Good God. Her firm, full body forced any other questions out of my mind and set my mouth to watering. She was right. There was ripe, and there was waste. And I didn't want to waste another moment talking.

We tumbled into the wall before collapsing on the floor, a tangle of arms and legs. Her jumper tore beneath my clawing fingers, our laughter mingled together like wild vines climbing up the walls. Our lips sought each other out like shadow and light.

Tonda pulled her lips away from my mouth, making me dizzy with want. She was incredible. Sweet, tart, smooth, salty. I could taste her, smell her and the dark, earthy juice of the cherries in her warm mouth.

"Can we move this to a bed? I'm all for adventure, but comfort does heighten pleasure. And I want to be oh so pleased tonight." Tonda tugged at my chin and rose up on her elbow.

Breathless, speechless, I simply nodded and shifted back on my haunches. Tonda took the hand I offered to help her up off the floor. She stood up and teasingly unzipped her jumper and stepped out of it, one slow, seductive leg at a time. Her smile gleamed bright as she watched me watching her.

"Bring some cherries. And the wine." She turned her back to my gaped open mouth and moved out of sight.

Back in the kitchen, I snatched at the carton of cherries, spilling a few across the counter. The wine bottle and glasses were awkward in my hand, clanking together as I tried to gather everything at once. The glasses tinkled together like a bell, and suddenly Sara's sweet smile flashed in my mind. *Such a sweet kid. Always so polite and helpful.* I wondered if she was off work yet.

"Are you coming or not?" Tonda called out. She'd obviously found the bedroom.

I shook Sara free from my mind and warned Tonda to get ready.

"Oh, I'm ready. Are you?" Spread across the bed like a lazy lioness, Tonda looked me up and down and licked her lips. Her gaze halted me at the door to my bedroom. Her seductive smile was sweet and soft for a moment, not unlike Sara's, which made her look all the more wicked.

"Come. Here." She purred. Thoughts of the sweet grocery store clerk fizzled just as quickly as they popped up.

"Demanding little thing, aren't you?" I teased.

"You'll learn to like it."

She took the wine and glasses from me, placed them on the nightstand, then jerked me toward her, laughing her infectious, sparkling laugh as some cherries spilled across the bed. I started laughing too, unable to help myself.

She de-stemmed two dark treats and popped them in her mouth. Without hesitation she kissed me and squirted the dark juice into my mouth.

"That's what it'll be like," she cooed against my lips, snagging my skin with her teeth. My body shivered so violently, I thought I might pass out. But Tonda took control, gripping my shoulders and climbing onto my lap like she'd done it a thousand times before. Her kisses landed wildly across my lips and chin, then up and down either side of my neck. She kissed and bit hungrily, no longer holding back.

"Ooh."

I flinched when her teeth caught me deep in the muscle.

"You're alright," she cooed and continued her nibbling. Her hands gripped my shoulders tighter, holding me captive against her. Her teeth sank in again, even deeper.

My cry of pain didn't stop her this time. She bit and sucked and soothed the sting until I felt like I was floating. My body drifted in one direction and my head another. *What is she doing to me? How?*

"Mmm."

I heard myself relaxing into Tonda's touches until I fell back onto the bed. Her sexy, toothy smile hovered above me, the ring around her pupils glowing a burnish red. I stared deep into those warm, welcoming eyes and realized she looked like a wild creature with an open mouth looming over me. Cherry juice painted her lips, and a bit dribbled over her chin. Her hands rubbed up and down my shoulders until finally I felt her tweaking my nipples one after the other, soft pinches followed by tight twists of her fingers.

"You like it," she whispered to me over and over again. And I did. The pain where she bit me was just a light throb. I wondered if I'd have a hickey. Would it show on my skin, all purpled and black? I'd never had a hickey before. The thought put a wide grin on my face.

...

I woke up the next morning feeling more hung-over than I ever had in my life. We hadn't drank that much— the bottle of wine sat half full on the nightstand. I sat up, and instantly laid back down as my bedroom started spinning. It took me several minutes to reclaim a steadier view. *Ugh!*

I was in bed alone, but evidence of last night was everywhere. Mashed up cherry skin stained the sheets, little brown pits were spat haphazardly on the floor, Tonda's jumper was crumpled up in the corner. *Where is she?*

I looked around and strained to hear if she was in the bathroom. I heard nothing. It was almost eerily quiet. Tonda was gone, but she lingered everywhere. Her smell, her presence, her heat. A wave of disappointment knotted my stomach, but the uneasy pang of confusion won out. If her jumper was still here, was she just traipsing around in her bra and panties? *Or maybe she borrowed something while I was asleep.* It took several moments for that thought to register and make me get out of bed. I shuffled over to my closet and pulled the door open. A quick perusal showed nothing was missing. I grinned a bit to myself. *Tonda would look crazy sexy in one of my dress shirts.* She appeared in my head, smiling widely and waving at me.

I'll see you soon, darling.

The sound of her voice rang in my head, like she was standing right behind me, but closer.

Damn, I am hung-over. I grinned to myself, half shuffling, half floating to the bathroom. I splashed water on my face without looking at my reflection. I didn't need to see the damage. I could feel how wrecked I was. I swung open the cabinet to find a remedy, but I was out of Alka-Seltzer.

A trip to the market was in order. Slipping on a pair of shorts and a T-shirt, I opted to walk to the grocery store in hopes the fresh air would help my hangover.

The sunlight felt good on my bare arms, each ray penetrating me. I could feel the energy jumping around inside me, filling me, lifting me off the ground. The breeze felt cool and smooth over my skin, like a whisper over my scalp, sending tingles skirting down my spine and reminding me of Tonda's touches. I longed to stand there for hours, as my nipples hardened with each caress of the air.

I'll see you soon, darling. There was her voice again. The wind carried it right up to my ear.

The automatic doors to the store opened before I even got close to them, as if they sensed my arrival. *Strange.*

The stale air filled my nose as I walked in, and I immediately felt a wave of nausea rock back and forth in my stomach. Cherries and wine burned the back of my throat, and my headache crashed back down on my temples. I needed to get back into the fresh air.

My attempt to quickly read the aisle signs knocked me off balance. *What the hell is going on? Before I came in here I felt like I could take on the world. Now I can hardly stand.*

I decided to go back outside. But that didn't happen.

Sara's bright energy was approaching me, and I found my fingertips warming and tingling the closer she got.

"Hey," she said, her voice was riddled with concern and surprise.

Her energy rolled toward me in bolts— it was almost too much. She reached out to pat me on the back and both my arms grew hot.

"Hey yourself. Whew!" I rocked forward on the balls of my feet trying to shake the overwhelming heat washing over me.

"Are you all right? I didn't think I was going to see you again." Sara's voice sounded so far away, her words crisp and hard. I stared at her for a long moment, registering our closeness. It didn't feel right. Her face was different, like she'd grown older overnight. Lines wrinkled her forehead and creased the edges of her eyes. *Why didn't she think she'd see me again?*

"What do you mean? You know I'm in here at least once a week. More if I forget things." She continued to stare, the most absent expression on her face. "What?"

"Nova, I've not seen you in a month. Not since you left with that, that woman. The pretty one."

"Huh?" Suddenly the front end of the store felt like it was on a tilt-a-whirl, spinning and pitching to and fro. The floor dipped and rose up in waves under my feet. "I was just in here last night, Sara. Last night."

Her face remained a blank wall, until she slowly shook her head back and forth. "No. Nova, that was a month ago. Nova, are you alright?"

Sara's hands reached out toward me as my legs buckled and I began falling. She caught me under the arms and held tight.

The lights were so bright all of a sudden, the sounds in the store grew louder and louder. The sprayer over the produce whooshed on, dousing leeks and cilantro in frigid water. Shopping cart wheels whined as they rolled across the freshly waxed floor. Even the sound of Sara's breathing echoed in my ears, a soft, rolling thunder. This was beyond hangover territory.

"You're all right," Sara said softly to me while soothing my shoulders. "You're going to be alright." Every time she patted me on the back or rubbed my shoulders, my fingers tingled and burned. I saw myself brushing fingers with Sara from the night before, her blushing and smiling. *Such a sweet kid.*

Panic needled up and down my legs. I looked up at Sara, needing to see those sweet, innocent eyes staring back at me. I was desperate for her to confirm she was still Sara and I was still Nova, just in need of Alka-Seltzer.

But looking back at me was Tonda, grinning widely. Her bright, white teeth were much sharper than I remembered, and they contrasted frighteningly with her dark skin, that now stretched harshly beyond the limits of Sara's features. *Something's very, very wrong.*

I gasped. A chill raced down my spine.

The spot where Tonda had sank her teeth into my skin began to throb and ache. I reached hesitant fingers to that side of my neck, now warm and sticky wet.

Two other clerks and another customer gathered around to help Sara position me upright against the wall. My head buzzed and swirled. I heard them murmuring. "Did she slip? Is she okay? Is that blood?"

I dabbed at my neck and looked at my hand. Thin, red drops dotted my fingers. I looked weakly from my hand up to Sara's face. Her lips moved, but it wasn't her voice.

"I'll see you soon."

Pretty

S. Andrea Allen

Everybody said she was pretty, for a fat girl. She was dark, too, but not so dark that people commented on her skin color. Ava guessed she probably *was* fat, kind of like Jill Scott before the first weight loss fat. Ava was a little shorter, and her boobs weren't quite as big as Jill's. Her weight had never come up until she had started dating women. She was sexy, too, and on more than one occasion women had mentioned her allure and attractiveness. And her eyes, they always loved her beautiful bedroom eyes. But none of that mattered; the woman she loved thought she was fat.

"I don't know what to do with a big girl," her lover had the nerve to say to one of Ava's friends. Her lover didn't have the balls to say it to her face, but she didn't seem to have any trouble at telling it to anyone else who would listen. Her lover also thought Ava was too femme, and for a while, she had tried to work on that: wearing more pants suits and less make-up, showing less cleavage and more attitude. Nothing worked. Even in a baseball cap and sneakers, Ava exuded femme energy. Her lover never did figure out that it wasn't about the clothes.

Ava liked her boobs. And she liked showing off the way her

breasts stood at attention and sat invitingly in her blouses and dresses. She always wore Cross Your Heart 18-hour bras so the girls would sit up just right. One of her friends said they looked liked bullets. Ava longed for a woman who would lean over and gently kiss the spot on her chest where her neck ended and the roundness of her breasts began. A woman whose mouth would water at the sight of her cleavage and the hint of tattoo that glistened when she wore just the right cut of blouse.

No matter, her lover didn't appreciate Ava's cleavage, or her femininity. It seemed strange to Ava; her lover also worked hard to hide her own masculinity. She had a bit of a dap to her walk. She said it reminded people of her father. She also loved to play basketball, and even coached a local women's team. But her lover also wore lots of make-up, so much so that she left greasy brown smears on anything that came into contact with her face. Her lover even wore skirts, mostly in conjunction with a tailored jacket, but a skirt nonetheless, and heels too! Ava didn't care about any of this (well, except the make-up stains on her clothes). It seemed to Ava that the "femme" wasn't the problem in their relationship; it was the fat.

For a while, Ava worked out at the new health club near the company both she and her lover both worked for. Even the janitor, Mr. Willie, noticed that her waistline was becoming more defined. Ava felt good about her appearance and she had gained a bit of confidence. Her lover always said she was too quiet and that people thought she was stuck up. Ava was shy, not stuck up at all, though she honestly didn't have much in common with the woman's friends other than the fact that they were all Black and lesbian. She supposed that should have been enough. Well, they had a little bit in common: Ava liked basketball, and so did her lover and her friends, and she also liked to play spades. They played nearly every night. Still, she never felt like she belonged in their crowd. They liked to gossip and fight in public, they were loud and rowdy, and slept with each other's girlfriends. But worse than that, none of them liked to read. Ava was a bookworm, and she loved to talk about politics and current events. She also loved to travel, but the only place these women wanted to go was to the liquor store and the club. They also liked to get drunk or high and talk about which straight woman they would turn out next.

Ava never could figure out why these women were attracted to straight women. There were perfectly nice (and single) lesbians all over town. Maybe it was the thrill of the chase, or the notion of pulling something over on the men the straight women were sleeping with. Who knew? But Ava thought it was dangerous. Didn't these women know about the soldier that had murdered his wife after he found out she was sleeping with a woman? Maybe that was why Ava didn't connect with the women. They liked to live life on the edge and Ava was more interested in staying alive and out of jail.

Ava liked her own friends just fine, most of the time. They could be a little petty and were constantly worried about look-ing "too gay." She wasn't quite sure what that meant at the time, but quickly realized that some of them had the same problem as her lover: they didn't want people to know they were lesbian. Again, Ava was confused. They fit all of the lesbian stereotypes: closely cropped hair, androgynous looking clothing, they even played softball for goodness sake! If gay had a look, they were it. Even though they tried to hide it, *everyone* on the job knew they were lesbian. They lived in a large town with a small mind, and everyone seemed to know everyone else's business. Even Ava's uber-religious parents knew she was lesbian, and though they didn't like it, they knew it to be the truth. Ava was pretty sure her friends' families knew the truth about them too.

Some of Ava's friends thought she was fat, too. But they also thought she was pretty, and smart. Her closest friend in the bunch, Kaitlyn, thought she was gorgeous, and loved to hug on her so she could feel on her "beautiful brown pillows." Ava didn't mind; it was all in good fun. Kaitlyn was also the one who reminded Ava that she wasn't fat at all. "Your curves are sexy. You shouldn't worry so much about what people think," she said. "Hell, some of us are fat too, some of us are even ugly." They had a good laugh about that one. Kaitlyn was the one who told her what her lover had said. It hurt, for a while, but Ava was beginning to figure things out. Ava was starting to think that perhaps she was indeed beautiful, curves and all, and that maybe her lover was the one with the problem. Her lover was always pretending that she was doing anything but laying up in the bed with Ava, and it seemed pretty ironic that she didn't have a problem with her fat then. Ava was also tired of overhearing her lover lying to her mother about where she was and who she was with. Tired of her pretending to have a boyfriend so the guys she did business with wouldn't call her a bulldagger behind her back. They did it anyway, but maybe her lover didn't hear them.

Ava was already out to her family and friends, and wasn't about to go back in the closet for anybody, not even the woman she had fallen in love with. Perhaps, Ava thought, it was time to fall more deeply in love with herself. She didn't need her lover's validation any more, not that she ever got it from her anyway. Her lover was nice to her, sometimes, but more often than not, she found something to criticize: her hair, her clothes, the length of her fingernails. Ava respected her lover's complexity, but couldn't remember why she had fallen for her. Each passing day revealed more tension, more discomfort with their relationship, and soon it became clear that love wasn't what she was feeling toward the woman anymore. She had fallen in love with possibility (she thought they'd make a good team), and her silky smooth voice. The woman had an amazing phone voice and when they would talk on the phone late at night, woooo weeee! Her panties got wet just thinking about it. Now, though, the woman's voice was crunchy, like gravel on an old dirt road.

That she had fallen out of love with the woman came as no surprise to Ava. She'd known that they were polar opposites, but she had tried to make the relationship work, for a while. It was clear that the woman had a problem with Ava's weight, but she also had a problem with her own identity, and while on some level Ava understood, she knew that she couldn't continue to be with a woman who didn't love her just the way she was. So, she called her up and asked, "Have you figured out what to do with a big girl?"

The woman was stunned into silence. She had no idea that her comments about Ava's weight had found their way to Ava's ears.

"No worries," Ava said. "You don't have to worry about it anymore. This big girl has figured out what to do with herself."

Missing
Lauren Cherelle

I like this part of the day. Sittin' at my little oak table watchin' the sun fall, restin' my limbs, listenin' to my husband talk and chew, and try to talk when he should be swallowin'.

James tell me all the things other women know and the things they husbands won't tell 'em. He don't want nobody ever thinkin' they can put one over on me. James say that's why he do it, 'cept I know it's more than that. My listenin' give him a chance to unload all the stuff he never wanna hear in the first place. He take a long breath then let me know that Mattie's youngest girl, Lilly, didn't come in last night.

James' youngest brother, Bo, sweet on Lilly, but the menfolk don't like her daddy, Willie, 'cause he done elected hisself a buffer between *us* and *them*. Willie done forgot that eyes can't look in two different directions.

"Willie come up to me right after I hitch that ole mule. Ain't got the decency to wait 'til a man standin' upright and lookin' him in the eye 'fore he start spoutin' fightin' words and accusin' Bo of runnin' off with his baby girl."

Ain't nothin' new 'bout Bo turnin' up missin'. He always

skippin' town on the back of some train with nothin' but a pair of dice and deck of cards in his pockets. James know Bo heart set on money, not some girl. Especially not some girl that's too shy and too skinny. The only reason James talkin' 'bout Lilly right now is 'cause of her momma. Folks love her 'cause she the sweetest lady in the county. But most folks loyal to her out of pity. Folks treat Mattie better than they own mommas hopin' it'll ease the burden of havin' to spend her life with that no count Willie.

James take another pass on his chicken bone before he toss it to his plate. He grab his napkin to wipe his hands clean. Like always, I get tickled when he do it 'cause it sound like he rubbin' against sandpaper. His hands rougher than tree bark 'cause day in and day out he handlin' rope and puttin' things together that don't go no more than oil and water. When the sandin' stop he look at me and say, "What'chu think?"

If Lilly was any other girl in Catahatchie County I would say she probably up and done what too many of us women only whispered 'bout when we was comin' up. But Lilly too careful 'bout what other folks say and do to just up and run off like that. She been 'round the same folks for all sixteen of her years but act like she just met us yesterday.

James ain't rushin' me for an answer, so I hike my skirt up and let the breeze seepin' in the windows kiss my skin for a spell before I move on to my next thought.

Now I done seen the way Bo look at Lilly, and I done see how Lilly look at Bo. She look at him like she choosin' what's left. And every week at Sunday School since Easter, I watch how Helen's girl look at Lilly, and I watch how Lilly look back. Lilly don't ever treat Helen's girl like a stranger.

"Mmm," come out first. Then I start to find words for my other feelin's.

Folks know 'bout my other feelin's. But James know better than all of 'em. My sister call my other feelin's a gift. "When

God don't bless women with chi'ren," she say, "he bless 'em with somethin' else."

When me and James first start neckin' downhill by the river, he asked me 'bout 'em. It's hard to put words to somethin' other folks ain't got, so I leaned back on that old cypress tree and told him what I still feel 'til this day. Sometimes when folks get near me or catch my eyes the right way, my hands start to shake and my blood get to movin' too fast. Make me sweat 'round the collar. And I get all these thoughts in my head I ain't think of. Then the thoughts drop to my mouth. And when I part my lips to let 'em out, folks buck they brown eyes and say I speak with God's breath. Then they hand me a quarter for the blessin'.

James ain't gone put no quarter in my palm but he still wanna hear my feelin's. I can't tell him 'bout the syrupy looks between Lilly and Helen's girl without tellin' him that these looks is natural with women. That it only take two seconds to look over and tell her what you want, how you want it, and where you wanna get it. James can't hear all that. 'Cause the next thing he gone say is "who the hell you been lookin' at?" and then he gone say "it's a sin 'fore God!"

He ain't gone understand how women feed each other even when we ain't got nothin' to give but a "morning" or "have mercy"— or how women stick to each other most right before we get pushed into the arms of a man.

I know them looks Lilly givin'. She done found comfort somewhere she can't settle. I don't need my other feelin's to tell me that's done happened. I done seen those looks since the day I was born, since the day I learned that's how my momma looked at Miss Emma.

Miss Emma was everything my momma was not. Gentle, slow to fuss, and crazy 'bout schooling. From the outside, they didn't have a reason to speak to each other, not even a reason to sit on the same pew. 'Spite all of that, one was bread and the other one butter. Momma's ways melted whenever Miss Emma showed up. She took the snap out her tongue and the swing out her hips. Didn't hit me what Momma was doing 'til I start doin' the same thing with James. Momma changed to stroke Miss Emma, to show her how much she was willing to bend in her direction.

Memories of Momma startin' to bring me down. I look at James so I can go on and answer him. He study his plate to make sure ain't no chicken left on the bones he done already wiped cleaner than the Virgin Mary. When he give up and look over I smile a little. My husband try his best to be a God-fearing man. Told me the night we married I'm more than his wife. "We ain't got much," he said, "but that don't mean I can't treat you like a rich lady. And when I can't do that, I'll treat you like my best friend. Promise you that."

I know James care 'bout my feelin's and such, but he don't really wanna hear 'bout the way of this world. So I'm gone say what he can handle: "Tell Willie the truth. Bo got a girl in every county from here to Miss'ssippi."

...

Ain't enough colored folk in the county to supply me with enough quarters where I can stay put and tend to my home every day. So I help James out by washin' and pressin' for Missus Abigail. She got me a little more work by callin' out to her friends. That's an extra seven-fifty a week. But I gotta do a lot more walkin' in the afternoon 'cause they houses stretch 'cross the county. But it ain't too hot out today 'cause it's late October and the weather dippin'. And once I go down Broad Street and cut through some fields, I'll be halfway home.

The closer I get to town the more church members I see. We speak but ain't got time for socializin'. Gotta hold off 'til Sunday. Lots of folks out cuttin' in front of me, movin' like they gettin' paid to rush. Seem like every time I come to town more and more trucks with stuffed beds drivin' through. And folks got more and more signs in they windows like we don't already know what they sellin'. I look ahead at my turn by the fillin' station and see Sheriff Dougherty at the jailhouse door speakin' to folks. I shole hope he don't say nothin' to me. This wash I'm carryin' too heavy for a break. I got another mile to go and my feet don't like stoppin'.

"Izola," he say long before I even get to where he standin'.

I get closer to the steps and stop in his direction, keepin' my eyes between his feet and shins. "You know anything 'bout this Lilly girl?"

"No, suh. Heard she missin'."

"When's the last time you seen her?"

"Thursday mornin' in Mister Simmons field."

"What you think happened to her?"

My eyes hurry to his face. Colored folk supposed to like this sheriff 'cause he don't bend with the wind or stand for no killin'. Back in the spring, a group of colored men from the big counties started comin' by both colored churches tryin' to get more of us to start votin'. "Can't get us on the ballot 'til we start votin' more," they say. "Don't matter that we ain't votin' for one of us right now." Well everybody know the new mayor and Sheriff Dougherty second cousins. And if we don't vote for 'em, they gone feel like we stealin' what everybody know is theirs. So the mayor and sheriff droppin' little favors here and there to sweetin' folks up before the next election. It ain't nowhere near election time, but they want somethin' in return every day. They expectin' all of us to supply 'em information even before they ask. And Willie and a handful of fools keep givin' it to 'em.

That's why I ain't a bit surprised Sheriff Dougherty outside pickin' and choosin' which colored folk he wanna speak to, or askin' me what I think 'cause he expect us to chirp like birds. But I can see in his pink, puffy face that he want more than a colored woman story. I ain't never sat down and shared my other feelin's with no white folk. Never will. But it's enough Willies 'round here for 'em to know what to expect from me.

I ain't got no reason to think somethin' done happened to Lilly. Every time I say her name or think of her little round face, I don't feel no tingling in my fingers. So I think she all right. If Lilly smart as I think she is, she done saved every spare penny she can keep her hands on. Why would Lilly wanna stay in this small box of a town where you can't step left or right without somebody sayin' you doin' it wrong?

I drop my eyes and say, "Young folks somethin' else nowadays. She out there thinkin' she can fly without her full-grown wings. Won't be surprised if I see her at church this Sunday."

"Humph," he respond and suck on his pipe. "All right then."

...

Lilly been missin' for nine days now. She didn't show up at church yesterday. Her momma didn't neither. Now I feel bad for not goin' to see Mattie so I can tell her not to worry 'bout Lilly and let her know that her family in my prayers every mornin', noon, and night. I wanted to wait before I went to see her 'cause I know all the women been in her face with they ideas of where Lilly at and why she left with no word. I ain't want Mattie to see me comin' and think I'm carryin' somethin' bad.

So I come home every evenin' to cook and wait for James to walk in. Between the waitin', all I do is step from the stove to the sink and back. And when I get to the sink I stare out the window up the road for my sister. She been stoppin' by every day to let me know what's happenin' with Mattie-nem. While she talkin', she help me peel potatoes or snap some peas or somethin'. She got a mother-in-law in her house that do all the cookin' so she don't mind helpin' me none. My sister talk all the way 'til James come before she cut through my garden and go back home. Then James sit in her place and tell me somethin' all the way different from what she done told me. I trust what James tell me, not my sister. Her stories get seasoned by too much of other folk's spices. But that don't mean I still don't wanna hear 'em.

I got my greens simmerin' down real good and the cornbread done. So I pull my apron off and get myself all ready to rest my feet since my sister takin' all day to come over. She don't live but two houses down but late like she live two miles away. Just when I'm fixin' to turn my back on the stove, lightin' hit the door and startle me. My sister done bust through the door so fast and loud I 'bout pee myself.

"Get to Mattie's. Now," she shout. "I'll stay and tell James where you gone."

My apron fall to the floor but I leave it there. I don't need to know what happened to Mattie. Just matter that she need me. I fly out the house and cut through the back past the smokehouse, marchin' in the direction of the Johnson's land. The sun settin' a little earlier each day, leavin' the sky a blurry mix of oranges and purples, but I got just enough time to get there before dark.

Soon as I clear the peach grove and hit the posts holdin' in Willie's horses, I see two of Mattie's boys sittin' on the porch tappin' sticks. Either somebody sent 'em out the house or they don't wanna hear what's goin' inside. They keep quiet and clear the porch for me. Only thing makin' noises is the creakin' wood at my feet. They eyes done already warned me that they momma in a bad way.

When I get inside, everything too plain and quiet. This the time of day you smell the work of a woman's hands. But ain't nothin' stirrin' but Mattie's oldest girl. She sittin' by the door holdin' one of her babies close. "Miss Izola," she say.

"Don't worry 'bout it," I tell her. She wanna catch me up on all the crazy things her momma been doin' and sayin'. She ain't gotta spend no time tellin' me what's burnin' her heart. "I'm gone work this out."

I go on and cut through the kitchen so I can get to the back room. Ain't no skillet on the stove or food sittin' out. The towel Mattie use to wipe down her dishes look like it's been dry for days. Mattie usually got some fresh biscuits in the middle of her table. But ain't nothin' there but a vase of dead daisies.

Soon as I step to the back room I can smell the sadness. My sister told me yesterday that Mattie ain't lettin' nobody keep the door open or raise the window. She wanna suffer just as bad on the outside as she feelin' on the inside. I knock and walk on in to find Willie standin' next to the bed tryin' to force water down her throat.

"Let her be," I say.

He look over his shoulder.

I raise my hands to my hips to let him know ain't gone be no discussion 'bout it.

He throw the glass on the side table, spillin' most the water on the floor. Then he walk past me smellin' like a hard day's work and cheap tobacco.

"And close the door," I tell him.

I drag the rocker closer to Mattie and take a seat. It's too dry to breathe or move about, but I'm gone have to put up with this heat for a bit. I undoes my top button and lift my skirt off my calves. Mattie pull her back higher up on the pillows and turn her eyes to me. Most of her body under a quilt and she sweatin' all over her face and neck.

"What you doin' to yourself?" I ask.

The room a little dark 'cause the lamp ain't turned up all the way. But I see her eyes get as wet as her face. I grab the cloth from the table and pat her tears before I move to the sweat.

"Zola," she say. "You been pretty since the day you was born. You ain't have to worry 'bout gettin' the runt of the litter.

I ain't never want that for my Lilly 'cause she smart and 'bout as pretty as you."

"Mattie. Don't—"

"I know my Lilly got a way 'bout her," she say louder then choke on her voice. She take a sip of the water I offer before she start again. "She got a way 'bout her folks don't understand. But she ain't deserve to die so young."

"Don't say that."

"She gone! I can feel it. And I don't need you or Willie tellin' me different. He ain't tellin' the truth 'bout nothin'. That's why I called you over." She squeeze her eyes tight. "Please, Zola. Tell me what happened to her."

I open my mouth with nothin' to say. Then I look at the window, preparin' to let Mattie know this the last night she smotherin' herself. Soon as I gather my skirt to get out the rocker, Mattie lean over and snatch my wrist.

Her touch make my legs go weak and I fall back hard to the chair. I use my other hand to grab the frame and steady myself. My eyes wide open but the room done went black. My feet still on the floor but everything from my chest up feel like it's risin' in the air. I keep tryin' to tell Mattie to let me go. Each word stuck in my head. I can't shove the words out or move my arms or legs. Only somethin' I feel down in my feet. I dig my toes in my soles and bear down hard as I can.

I can't tell if I moved anything. Just feel tightness in my wrist. Then the colors come, dark and hazy. And something cold and soft touch my ears and the room sound different. I can't hear Mattie breathin' no more. Everything sound deep, like I done pushed my head under water. I don't see nothin' but flashes of green and brown. Something hard start pressin' in the back of my head and I can barely push my chest out to take a full breath.

The colors fade away and I feel like I'm gone come out of this 'til a rush of water hit my chest and start creepin' up my neck.

I turn my head the little bit I can 'cause I don't want to drown. That don't do nothin' but push the colors away. They break up and start to show somethin' I know I don't wanna see. I can't tell what it is; too many sticks and rocks and leaves movin' 'round it. But the water slowly pushin' the dirty mess my way. Soon as a tangled bunch of them sticks go over my head I see her face.

Lilly face make me scream and the water rush in and hush me. My chest heavin' hard and I can't hold on to my strength. I can't find no part of me to fight off this bad dream Mattie done pushed me in. I don't wanna see Lilly like this. Her skin peelin' off her swollen face and she driftin' in a cloud of red. Her bulged eyes ain't nothin' but soft gray. And her mouth startin' to come open and poke somethin' narrow out. It move up her lip and show its slick head. The snake push her lips back to drag its thick body out her mouth. The silver between its brown scales start to glow and do somethin' to me. The itchin' start at my finger nails and shoot up my arms. And my skin pullin' so tight 'round my arms that it dry up and crack. The stingin' makin' me weak but I can't stay on the pain 'cause the snake out of Lilly body and swim- min' right to me. I force my lips together so hard feel like they bleedin' on my teeth.

I can't let the snake in me. So I bear down to find my weight in the chair. I can feel the wood on the back of my legs but it ain't no use. I can't break away. Ain't go no fight left in me. I close my eyes and wait for the snake to touch me. I can't even hold my head up to know when it's gone get me. My throat burnin' and I feel myself slumpin' over. I thought I'd be sinkin' deeper into the water, but now I don't feel it on my neck. The water fall past my waist. I start catchin' my breath and pushin' it out at a better rhythm. Then colors give way to the black I usually see behind my eyes.

Soon as I feel my hands tremblin', I lift 'em up real fast and rub my arms down to make sure I'm right again. My skin ain't cracked but it's still stingin'. And everything on me dry except my chest.

"Tell me," Mattie say, her voice breaking. "I need to know."

I push myself up 'til I hit the back of the chair. Then I wipe sweat from my neck and raise my achin' head. That's when the vision start to speak to me.

I can't tell Mattie that her daughter in a filthy grave at the bottom of the Catahatchie River. I can't tell her that her youngest son caught Lilly and Helen's girl feelin' under each other's dresses behind the school buildin'. Or that her son snitched to Willie right after. Then Willie tried to force James to find his brother and marry Lilly. And when Lilly caught wind of what was happenin' she decided to go. But Willie caught her in the yard fixin' to leave home for good, and in the heat of the moment, hit the girl so hard she fell back and knocked her head on the well pump. Force of the fall popped her neck in a bad spot. She died in the wet grass right at his feet. And 'stead of Willie takin' the blame for her death, he found someone to help get her body to the river without notice. Promised long as her body don't come afloat, he'll pay or do whatever for a lifetime of silence.

I can't tell Mattie who put her there, but I can tell her why it happen. I look in her sick eyes, gently take her moist hands and say, "The Lord shoulda given us smaller hearts if we can't use 'em where we see fit."

I leave Mattie wailin' and shoutin', cursin' Willie and fightin' her eldest off. Gone take a while before she find peace. But it's best this way. She don't need to know word-for-word what happen 'cause it won't do nothin' but turn her kind heart bitter.

So I let her be and follow my path back home. The walk gone be long 'cause I'm draggin' my feet. My body wore out from bein' used and the back of my head still hurtin'. Take everything in me not to lose my footin'.

When I get home, I use what little strength I got left to go to the fence past the smokehouse, then fall to my knees to start pullin' rotted boards off the heap James ain't burned yet. I can't see much of nothin' out here in the dark, but my hands know what they doin'. I'm careful with the boards so I won't catch a splinter. A foot below the scraps I feel what I'm searchin' for. I wrap my fingers 'round the hardened laces and use my other hand to push my knees out the dirt.

I slide my feet inside the house and close the door behind me. James in the kitchen, chair square with the door, waitin' for me. His eyes ain't met mine yet. They still fixed on the boots danglin' from my hand. The boots heavier than they should be 'cause they caked-up with red mud from the banks of the Catahatchie.

James sittin' so still seem like he scared to move and face what he tried to hide from me. I toss the boots 'cross the kitchen, aimin' just right so they land at his feet. Soon as they fall the mud crack off, leavin' a mess on the floor I shined last week. "You better hope the Lord don't think more 'bout the dirt at your feet," I say.

I push off on my left heel 'cause it don't hurt as much as the other one and go to the bedroom. I lay on top of the bed, shoes and all, and ask the Lord to lend me some of the peace Mattie gone find one day.

...

The days get shorter and the weeks get colder as they should. I open the stove so the heat can fill the house while me and James eatin'. We sit at the table and rest with the radio low, but James' tellin' and my listenin' ain't the same. I used to hang on to his words. And in the moments of quiet a little nod or laugh would bring us close. Ain't no more easy talkin'. He mull over his words to figure out what parts he gone wait and tell. And between the waitin' he barely speak.

I push my hips out to get more comfortable in my seat and

think 'bout all the folks who done heard me say, "Don't matter if you pulled the trigger. You heard the shot, so that make you a witness."

I knew the night James sat at this table and said Willie accusin' Bo of runnin' off with Lilly that somethin' wasn't right 'bout the story he was tellin'. I shoulda trusted in the Lilly I knew and stopped the lie right then 'stead of lettin' James paint somethin' different. I let my husband plant a seed that was supposed to kill a truth that was already in me. I didn't wanna see Lilly in the river where I first let James love me. I didn't wanna bear witness to what had already happened. I ignored the shot. I swallowed what I know 'bout the way of people so my other feelin's wouldn't come between me and my husband.

James used me once. He know I ain't gone let him do it again. I can't listen without keepin' my eyes on him. And when I'm watchin', he stop talkin' altogether. He tell me things now just to see what parts I know already, to see what parts of me ain't no different than Lilly.

Trim
La Toya Hankins

Trim got around. It seemed that every time she and I went out to the grocery store, to the club, hell, even when we went to church, women would come up and drawl, "Hey Trim," with an embarrassingly large smile. When that happened, Trim would do her sly grin and drawl out, "Hey baby, how are you doing?" She would then snatch them up in a hug and whisper something in their ear that would cause them to blush and say, "Trim, you so nasty."

Trim, or Trimeka Rochelle, and I had been friends since grade school. We had the typical fights early on in the schoolyard that sprang from "I-heard-you-told-somebody-you-wanted-to-fight-me." The novelty of that soon wore off when we started spending too much time in after school detention. We went through high school graduation, college separations, and sexual frustrations and the bonds of our friendship grew stronger with each trial.

We considered ourselves to be such good friends that, after getting our degrees and finding jobs in the same city, we decided to share an apartment. Everything was cool, until *she* showed up, and things haven't been the same since.

"Excuse me, I hate to bother you, but I just moved in across the hall and my telephone isn't hooked up yet. May I borrow yours to check on when my furniture will be arriving?" this 5' 4" caramel-colored cutie with a reddish-brown natural asked as she stood in the apartment doorway.

I adjusted the grocery bags in my hand to unlock my apartment door. I motioned her in while introducing myself.

"Nice to meet you Katie. I'm Sharon," she said as I closed the door and showed her where the telephone sat on the coffee table.

"No, K.D. like Katherine Diana," I yelled from the kitchen. "I go by my initials."

"That's cute. Like K.D. Lang, right. I love her music."

A sister who knew about the Canadian cowboy chanteuse? That was interesting. Walking back into the living room, I saw an apple-shaped rear covered in FUBU jeans pointed toward me while the other end of Sharon pointed toward the stereo.

"They have me on hold so I was admiring your record collection."

"Half of the CDs are my roommate's. The ones that are jazz and R&B are mine. The rap and dance music are hers."

"So you are the fan of Ella Fitzgerald and Etta James and she's the fan of Eve and Eazy-E."

"Right," I said with a smile. "Do you want something to drink?"

"No, thank you. I know as I soon as I take a sip that's when someone will answer the phone."

"Well, don't say I didn't offer. If you need me, I will be in the back working on my computer. I have a project I need to finish by tomorrow."

"What kind of project, if you don't mind me asking?" Detailing the package I was putting together for my design company to bid on a government project, Sharon seemed really interested. Her brown eyes followed my every word. I had to admit, it was a slight ego boost to have such a beautiful person think what I had to say was interesting. Before I could delve too much into my life story, the person on the other line answered so I headed to my room to finish working on the project.

After fifteen minutes, Trim's rich alto filled the apartment as she announced she was home from another day in the salt mines. I walked down the hall to say hello and introduce the two of them, only to find Sharon and Trim locked into looks that didn't seem too friendly on either side.

"Trim, this is our new neighbor Sharon. Sharon, this is my roommate Trim."

In a monotone as flat as the shoes she wore to teach third grade Trim answered, "Hello."

The mutual dislike in the room was thick enough to be cut and served on toast. With a sidelong glance at me, Trim went down the hall to her room and closed the door. Sharon just rolled her eyes and reached for her purse after hanging up the phone.

"Thanks again for the use of the phone. The guy said the furniture delivery people should be here any moment. They took a wrong turn on the interstate and got lost. So I will be heading over to my place. Feel free to drop by anytime."

"Thanks for the offer. I will keep that in mind."

"Good luck on your project."

"Thanks and welcome to the neighborhood," I said, opening the door and waiting until she unlocked hers.

At the sound of our door closing, Trim came back into the living room wearing a North Carolina Central T-shirt and Johnson C. Smith shorts.

"What the hell was Sharon doing here using the phone?"

"She moved in across the hall and needed to use it to check on her furniture arriving. How do the two of you know each other?"

"I met her last summer at a seminar in Chicago. We had a few drinks, a roll in the hay and it was over."

"Okay," I said sitting on the couch as Trim sat beside me and turned on the television.

"Most of the times when you run into your one-night stands there isn't nearly as much shade as I just witnessed."

Turning to a cooking show Trim responded, "After Chicago, we kept in touch through phone calls and e-mails. She seemed to think that it was more than it actually was so I had to put her in her place a few months back when she started talking about making a commitment."

"You don't think she moved here to still try to get with you, do ya?"

"No. Sharon was looking for a gig here when we met in Chicago. That's how we started our conversation. She asked me about good places to stay and I suggested this place because of the location and the price."

"Still, don't you think it's strange that she ended up moving across the hall?"

"Please, I'm not thinking about her. Trust me, after the letting down I gave her, I'm sure living across from me on purpose was probably the farthest thing on her mind."

"Okay, if you say so."

During the course of the next two months, I saw Sharon occasionally at the mailbox, or leaving her apartment when I was came into mine, or vice versa. Each time, we exchanged brief, pleasant conversation but nothing of any real substance.

So it came as a big surprise when three months after our initial meeting, I bent down to pick up the daily newspaper one morning along with a handwritten note, inviting me over that night for dinner and drinks, courtesy of Sharon.

Not one to turn down an offer of hopefully good company and good food, I slipped a note under her door stating I would be over around 8 p.m.

That night, over homemade vegetable lasagna and two bottles of wine, we shared a lot about each other and a lot of laughter. During our conversation, we shared we were single and not really into going out to clubs to meet someone special.

"You know what K.D., I like you. You're funny, smart, and enjoy my cooking. We should really hang out more," Sharon said.

"I agree. I had fun tonight with you. It's not often enough that I find someone who loves Zora Neale Hurston books and vampire movies almost as much as I do."

Sharon slowly smiled. "So I guess we are going to be more than just neighbors now?"

After taking a sip of my wine, I leaned over and answered with a passionate kiss to confirm we were an item.

At first, Trim didn't have anything to say about Sharon and I dating, which I found a little surprising. We have never dated someone who had dated the other first. Still, no words passed from Trim's lips about the matter. I figured she was good. However, after the scent of the flowers that Sharon kept sending to me began filling the house, and I began to spend more time across the hall than at home, the little comments started.

"That girl called and left you a message."

"Are you staying home tonight or are you going elsewhere?"

"In case you have forgotten, because it seems you are never here anymore, the rent is due next week."

I took everything in stride but the final straw came one night when Sharon was running late from work. I was chilling at home in my robe. Sharon and I were going out to a jazz club and I was in no rush to put on the foundation garment that gave me that killer silhouette.

"Excuse me. Do I know you? You look vaguely familiar. Have we met before?" Trim asked as she walked in from her weekly Tai Chi class. Her ebony face wore a slight smirk as she passed me and went into the kitchen to get herself a drink of juice.

"Ha-ha very funny. I happen to live here, remember?"

"Could have fooled me. Seems like you live across the hall with that bitch from the Windy City."

"Hold up, I'm not going to let you call my girl out her name. Apologize."

Walking down the hall, she paused in front of her bedroom and said, "No!"

I just sat there for about five minutes waiting for her to change her mind and do the right thing by begging for my forgiveness. When that didn't happen, I jumped up and stormed into Trim's room. I was prepared to kick ass and take names— until she pulled off her sweatpants. During the time we lived together, I had never seen Trim's body unclothed. I stood in awe of her perfectly round breasts. Her plump nipples resembled chocolate covered cherries. Her breasts sat triumphantly above a tight stomach. The dove tattoo she got when she joined her sorority looked even better than I imagined. I was speechless. Besides the flat stomach, Trim had the proverbial wide hips that made lesbians moist at the thought of caressing them. Added to that, her pubic hair formed the shape of a heart. I had never seen such a perfectly shaped body and here I was about to curse it out.

"What? Did you come in for something? I know you didn't come in here to make me apologize."

"Actually I was… I mean… I came in here for that purpose."

"Well you'll be in here by yourself because I'm not saying I'm sorry." She brushed past me for the shower.

I stepped forward to grab her arm. "You are not going to get off that easy. I kicked your ass in grade school for calling my momma a bitch and I can kick your ass now for calling my lady a bitch."

"But you forget, K., I was about a hundred pounds lighter and a lot shorter then," Trim said, pushing me into the wall.

We banged up and down the wall of the hallway into the living room. In the middle of our rolling around my robe came off, then it was skin against skin. First, Trim was on top of the fight then I was. As I wrangled my way on top of her, the phone rang. I knew it was probably Sharon but my hands were full with Trim. I started feeling a little light headed as Trim's hard nipples rubbed against my chest. Every time her flesh came in contact with mine I felt bursts of electricity shooting up and down my body. I sensed tension in Trim's body as my rock-hard clit kept bumping her leg but I had to avoid her pinning me on the carpet. I was a little bit embarrassed about being excited at the thought of wrestling with my best friend in the defense of my girlfriend, but damn, Trim's body felt good. She laid on top of me, holding my wrists down with her arms and her legs resting on mine. Struggling to catch her breath, Trim looked into my eyes.

"I told you I wasn't going to say I'm sorry," she said. Those were the same words she had said the last time we fought. Laid on the carpet, I realized I had lost that one too. But instead of getting up, Trim stayed on top of me. She still held my wrists but her grip was looser. Her body felt a little bit more relaxed. Traces of the essential oil she wore every day collaborated with her natural scent to envelop me with a sensory stimulant. Instead of getting up and taunting me with her victory, she seemed content to drape my body. Not knowing what else to do, I kissed her. Yes, I kissed her and it tasted like liquid sunshine mixed with a splash of bliss.

Slowly, she kissed me back, gently parting my lips to insert her tongue, causing my closed eyes to twitch with excitement. Trim kissed me with passion. I felt my soul was expanding each second our lips connected. Distantly, it seemed the phone began ringing again. The auditory intrusion didn't stop Trim from kissing my neck. Pausing to gently brush her lips at the hollow of my throat, Trim discovered my right breast. Latching on to my nipple, she paid tribute by sucking and licking it. She urged it to grow hard in her mouth and my backbone felt like melted chocolate. Not wanting to leave my left one out, she moved on to the west side and did the same thing. I felt like I had ascended to Mount Olympus to sit among the gods. The pleasure Trim was giving me was an inch beyond comprehension.

Moving up to kiss my neck again, I took advantage of the moment to demonstrate my skill set. I had always been told that I had a nasty wiggle. I wrapped my legs around Trim's back and took us on the ride of both our lives. On the floor, in front of the picture of us posing at our high school graduation with our parents, holding our diplomas, Trim shimmied along with me until— with a great shudder that split the world apart— we came. Opening my eyes I saw my best friend staring down at me. I just smiled. She smiled back and mouthed, "I'm sorry."

She rolled off of me and I crawled to the phone.

"Sharon, hey it's me. I'm sorry I missed your call a few minutes ago. Trim and I had some roommate business to discuss… No, I don't think I'm going to make it over tonight. We have a lot more stuff to take care of that just can't be put off any longer… I'll talk to you later."

That night was four months ago. I think that Sharon still lives across the hall. Between my job and Trim, I don't get out that much. Then again, Trim seems content to spend her nights at home with me doing "roommate business." When we do go out, the ladies recognize they need to keep their distance instead of expecting hugs.

And yes, Trim is that nasty.

The Other Side of Crazy
Eternity Philops

"It's not as bad as you think."

"Yes, the fuck it is!"

"Girl, you need to relax. Sit down and think this through."

It was one in the morning. My best friend, Lenore, had come over after I called her ranting about my girlfriend. She was doing her best to calm me down, but unfortunately her best wasn't good enough.

"How the hell am I supposed to 'relax,' L? She's still cheating on me!" I was pacing back and forth across the room. I felt like a caged animal, ready to run but no way to escape. I wanted to throw something against the wall, but I had enough sense not to break any of my own shit.

"You don't know that, Delilah. And you shouldn't waste energy getting upset unless you're sure." Lenore was always the levelheaded one. No matter how distraught I got, she stayed logical. I wish I had those qualities, but since I didn't, having Lenore was the next best thing. Or at least having her would be, if I ever listened to her.

"Okay, you're right. I *don't* know she's cheating." I stopped pacing and grabbed my car keys from the side table. "So I'll just go and get proof!"

"That's not what I meant, Delilah, and you know it!" Lenore hurried after me as I stomped through the front door.

It was 30 degrees in the dead of winter, but I didn't care; my anger was enough to keep me warm inside my flannel pajama set. Not the sexiest nighties, I know, but this wasn't a booty call. Lenore had the sense to throw a coat over her sweats and tank top. With her slender, petite frame, I always joked that she didn't have enough meat on her bones to make half a sandwich. I, on the other hand, had enough for a potluck supper plus some leftovers. But I've always been comfortable in my plus-size body, and tonight I was going to throw all 200 pounds and 5 foot, 6 inches of it at Sam and whatever whore she was fucking behind my back.

Lenore hopped into the passenger seat as I started the car. "Come on, Delilah. You're better than this: showing up at some woman's home in the middle of the night ready to fight."

"Oh, really? Since when? Because you know I've never been one to let someone come in and take what's mine." We were headed down Independence Boulevard toward Matthews. Sam lived only 10 minutes away, so she knew I could pop up at any time. But that minor distance seemed to also be a minor detail to her because I'd caught her with women over her house before, and was certain I would again tonight. The thought of it increased both my anger and my speed. Lenore, bless her heart, was still trying to talk me into going back home.

"Delilah, this isn't the way to handle this, like some ghetto hood rat. Your mama raised you with more class than this."

"My mama also raised me not to take any silly ass shit or game-playin'. In fact, that was life lesson number one. So I'm going over there and showing Sam exactly what I learned."

When we got to Sam's subdivision, I went into creep mode to make sure she wouldn't hear me coming. I cut off my headlights and slowed down to about five miles per hour. Except for the dull rumble of my engine, the neighborhood was silent. I was certain I'd find an unfamiliar car parked next to Sam's black Lexus coupe. Instead, I pulled up to a deserted house with an empty driveway.

"Where the fuck is she!" I screamed, pounding the steering wheel. I instantly pulled out my cell phone and dialed Sam's number. My call went directly to voicemail, so either the phone was off or she sent me there. I hung up and continued to empty my rage on the steering wheel. I beat it until the honking horn started to wake the neighbors. I saw a light go on in a near-by house.

"If you're done with your tantrum, maybe we should leave before someone calls the cops," Lenore suggested. I cut my eyes at her for calling my well-deserved ire a tantrum, but turned the car around and headed home.

As we rode in silence, I thought about all of the many places in Charlotte that Sam could be. Hell, she could be with some bitch across state lines in Rock Hill! In the past, I'd never been one to keep tabs on my woman. I didn't have to: my former girlfriends knew better than to mess with a good thing like being with me. But Sam? Sam was cocky. A local but well-known model photographer, I first spotted her at a fashion show. While everyone else had their eyes trained on the beauties sashaying down the runway, my eyes were on the caramel-skinned woman behind the camera. The seamless struts of the catwalk were just jagged gestures compared to the fluid movements of the photographer as she worked around the stage. I watched her the entire evening. Her lens may have been pointed at those models, but it was my heart that she captured with every click of her camera shutter, and by the end of the night I was determined to be the only woman she had in focus. So determined, in fact, that I didn't bother to wait for her to notice me. As soon as the show was over I walked right up to her and asked her out. Of course, at the time I didn't know Sam fancied herself a little player, though it probably wouldn't have mattered even if I did. As soon as I'd laid eyes on that woman, I knew I wanted her. And despite everything she put me through, I hadn't looked away since.

I nudged Lenore awake when we got back to my place. Watching her rub her eyes like a toddler, I realized just how late it was. Guilt took the place of my earlier anger.

"Girl, I'm sorry I dragged you into this mess tonight. You should have stayed your butt at home instead of coming here dealing with my crazy bullshit."

Lenore let out a wide yawn. "You mean dragging me into your mess 'this morning.' It's almost three a.m." She fished her keys out of her pocket. "But you don't have to apologize. This is what I live for, dealing with your crazy bullshit."

I gave Lenore a weak smile as she got out of the car. I truly did appreciate her always being there for me. She'd popped into my life in my late teens, and we'd been inseparable ever since, attending the same college and even moving together to Charlotte after graduation. It was a wonder that we'd never gotten together as a couple, but neither of us had ever felt drawn to that. Our friendship alone was fulfilling. Recently, Lenore had been away, and I'd felt a gaping hole in my life without her. But she was finally back home, back with me where she belonged.

"I'll call and check on you tomorrow," Lenore said with another yawn. I nodded, and with a wave she turned and walked toward her home a few houses down from mine. I sat in the car a few more minutes to watch her get home, but with my anger simmering down I was beginning to feel the biting chill of the winter air. Knowing she was safe, and feeling my rage-induced energy fading, I went back into the house, re-settled myself for sleep, and crawled into bed.

My thoughts began to drift to Sam and her trifling ways. I started wondering where she was laying her head, but shut my mind down before I lost my temper and started my tirade all over again. No, I'd rest and think things through after some sleep. Sam may have been out of reach for the night, but I had something for that cheating ass, most definitely.

...

I awoke later that morning with a sense of calm that had evaded me hours earlier. I was going to confront Sam—that hadn't changed—but I wasn't going to be that same belligerent, combative woman that drove to her house. My emotions were under control, and I'd handle Sam in a cool and sophisticated manner. Lenore would be proud.

What I did learn from last night was that showing up at Sam's place didn't guarantee I'd find her. But her office was another matter. Sam was a committed work-a-holic. If she was going to be anywhere, she'd be at her studio. I checked the time. It was only 9:30 a.m. I was supposed to be at work myself but I'd taken the morning off for a doctor's appointment. It was a routine appointment, so missing it wasn't a big deal. Still, I'd at least have to call to reschedule it if I wanted to avoid a late cancelation charge.

"Good morning, Dr. Harvell's office. This is Tina. How may I help you?"

"Good morning, Tina. This is Delilah Patterson. I have a ten-thirty appointment today but I'm going to need to reschedule it." I cradled the phone on my shoulder so I could get out of my nightclothes while I talked.

"Oh, Ms. Patterson. Please hold on while I give Dr. Harvell your message." The soothing tones of Kenny G played through my earpiece while I waited. I was naked and ready to shower by the time someone came back to the line. I expected to hear Tina give me some available dates, but was surprised to hear the burly voice of my doctor.

"Good morning, Ms. Patterson. Tina tells me you need to reschedule your appointment."

"Yes, that's right. I've had a personal situation arise and I can't make it this morning. I was calling so I could avoid the late cancelation charge, but since it's the day of and an hour away, I understand if I still have to pay it."

"No, that's not a problem. I just wanted to speak with you directly and make sure everything is okay." This was why I liked Dr. Harvell. He came from a generation that believed in friendly and personal service.

"Yes, everything is fine. I can come in sometime next week if you have any availability."

"For you, Ms. Patterson, I will always make the time. I'll give the phone back to Tina and she will schedule you. In the meantime, you keep up your regimen and call me if you need to, okay?"

I smirked. It was almost like speaking to a kindly, old grand-father.

"I'll see you next week, Dr. Harvell." Tina came back on the line and set my appointment for the upcoming Monday. I hated I'd have to use my personal time again to take off another morning, but this thing with Sam simply had to be dealt with.

After a quick shower I got dressed in one of my favorite outfits; a basic scoop-neck black dress that hugged my shape in all the right spots, complemented with some ruby red stilettos and a matching jewelry set. Looking good on the outside always made me feel better on the inside. Plus, I wanted Sam to see all this deliciousness she was risking with her unfaithful ways. I primped my close-cut, spiked hair, applied my MAC make-up, and headed to Sam's photography studio.

She'd recently moved her studio to an office building in the Uptown area. It was one of those buildings with front-desk security that made every visitor sign in, no matter what. Annoying as hell. I'd been here plenty of times and knew most of the staff. Today, however, I spotted a new face behind the desk. He was a young guy, couldn't be older than 22 or 23, and extremely cute, with one of those baby boy faces. If I was into men, I'd definitely be interested. Too bad for him I wasn't. Still, it was always good to be friendly, especially with the security guys. I walked up to the desk and flashed my pearly whites before speaking.

"Hi there, cutie. I'm here to see Samantha Greene. She's got a photography studio here."

"Good morning, ma'am." Baby Boy's dimples showed as he returned my smile. "Do you have an appointment with Ms. Greene?"

"No, I don't, but she knows me."

Baby Boy picked up the phone and dialed an extension. After about half a minute he hung up the phone.

"No one is answering. I think she's out."

Damn, first she wasn't home and now she wasn't at work. Maybe this was worse than I thought.

Baby Boy stroked his chin and thought for a few seconds. "Oh yeah, I remember, I saw Ms. Greene leave a little while ago. Said something about an early lunch meeting at that fancy steakhouse off College Street. If you want I can take a message for you."

I let out a small sigh of relief while keeping the smile plastered on my face.

"No, that won't be necessary. I'll just catch my girlfriend there. Thanks, cutie."

Baby Boy's eyebrows raised at my use of the word "girlfriend." Before he could respond, I turned and walked out of the building. On my way out he picked up the phone again. I overheard him say, "She said she's her girlfriend." I wasn't even out of earshot yet and he couldn't wait to tell his buddies about the lesbians. Typical man.

College Street was only a few blocks away and I knew what "fancy" restaurant Baby Boy meant, so I pulled my coat tighter around me and opted to walk. Despite the cold weather it was a beautiful day with a clear, blue sky, a rarity for the typical gray-toned southern winter. As I walked, I focused on Lenore's advice about not jumping to conclusions. Maybe Sam had a lunch meeting for work, networking with a model or another photographer or something. Maybe she *wasn't* creeping around behind my back. Maybe she *wasn't* dining with some bitch she was seeing on the side. Maybe it really was just business.

And then I saw her through the window. Both of them.

Sam was sitting across from a stunning, chocolate-skinned woman wearing a form-fitting orange turtleneck, boot-cut jeans, and black boots. Her shoulder-length locs were tied back with an orange and black, African print scarf. Even sitting down I could tell she was tall, at least 5'8", and no bigger than a size four. I couldn't see her too clearly through the glass, but I saw enough. She was, in a word, stunning.

Sam sat opposite her, and was wearing her trademark black slacks, long-sleeved black collared shirt, and black loafers. She wasn't an overly stylish woman, but Sam had such a handsome and confident air about her that she didn't need flashy clothes. My Sam had swagger.

And my Sam had another woman's hand in hers, caressing it slowly and affectionately.

I was beyond feeling wrath. I felt like I was in the eye of a hurricane. Everything within me was completely still. That is, until Sam leaned in and planted a kiss on the woman's lips.

I hit category five. All hell was about to break loose!

I had my hand on the handle of the restaurant door when my phone rang. I knew the ringtone; it was Lenore. Like the godsend that she was, she'd called at exactly the right moment.

"What's going on, Delilah?" Her voice full of concern. My own cracked under the pressure of the despair I was feeling.

"She's with another woman, Lenore! I'm standing outside the restaurant they're at. I watched them through the fucking window!" My hand was still on the door handle, awaiting my decision.

"Delilah, don't do anything rash. I know you want to go in there and beat the shit out of her, but you're better than that."

"Why does she keep doing this to me? Why can't I be enough for her?" My eyes begged to cry, but I refused.

"I don't know, honey. But you go in there and do what I know you want to do, and it'll hurt you more than it hurts her."

I took a deep breath and let go of the door. "You're right, Lenore. You're always right. I don't know why I keep letting her treat me like this. Any other woman I'd just walk away, but dammit, I love Sam so much!"

"If you're not going to walk away from the relationship, at least walk away from the restaurant," Lenore instructed. "Don't cause a scene there. It's just not a good look."

By now I was walking back toward Sam's office building. "I know. I already left. We're going to handle this in the privacy of her home."

"How are you going to pull that off?" Lenore asked. "You tried that last night and she wasn't there."

"This time she will be," I said with certainty.

"Oh shit. What are you planning, Delilah?"

"Don't worry. I'm not like I was last night. Yeah, I'm hurt. Hell, I'm pissed the fuck off. But I got this. I'm in control."

Lenore was doubtful. "I'm not buying that crap."

"I promise you," I assured her, "I'm calm. But if you want to make sure I don't go off the handle, just meet me at Sam's place. I'll be on my way there in a few minutes."

"Fine. Just wait for me in the car and don't do anything until I get there."

With that Lenore hung up, and I was back inside the office building. Baby Boy was still at the front desk. He gave me a nervous grin as I walked up to the counter.

"I'm sorry, ma'am. Ms. Greene still hasn't come back yet."

"I know. I want to leave her a message this time."

Baby Boy hesitated a moment. "I...guess that will be okay." He got a pen and pad ready.

"Just tell her that Delilah will be waiting for her at home."

Baby Boy raised a questioning eyebrow. "At home?"

I rolled my eyes. My friendly demeanor had been replaced with impatience.

"Yes," I confirmed curtly. "At home."

"Okay," he said, jotting down the message. "I'll give it to her as soon as she gets here."

"You do that." As I left the building a dull overcast began to cloud the sky. The beautiful blue, much like my emotional ease, had been short-lived.

...

When I pulled up to Sam's house this time the empty driveway didn't faze me. Nor did the fact that I didn't have a key, or at least not a legitimate one. The brick sitting in my passenger seat was all I needed. I'd told Lenore that I'd wait for her in the car, but I'd changed my mind. I was going to show Sam she couldn't do me any kind of way and think there wouldn't be consequences. I wasn't one of her little feeble-minded models who hung on her every word. Coming home to find me sitting in her living room was the way to remind her who the hell she was dealing with.

After making sure no one was nearby, I got out of the car and casually walked to the front door. I took another quick look around, then smashed the brick through the windowpane closest to the doorknob. I cringed as the glass shattered. Even at my angriest I'm not the type to hurt somebody or tear stuff up, no matter how much shit I talk. And despite her transgressions, I did feel bad about damaging Sam's house. No matter how things ended tonight, I'd reimburse her for the damage. Unlike her, I took responsibility for my actions, the good and the bad.

I checked to make sure no one had noticed the minor destruction I'd caused, then reached through the opening, undid the deadbolt and knob lock, and let myself in. I didn't know how long it would take for Sam to get my message from the front desk, so I took off my coat, turned on the wall-mounted television, and made myself comfortable on the sectional. It wasn't long before I heard Sam's engine in the driveway. Shit was about to go down.

"Delilah, what the hell are you doing in here?" Sam hollered as she barged through her front door. She took in the gaping hole in the pane and glass on the floor, and scowled at me. "You fuckin' broke my window!"

Standing up, I ignored the accusation and stayed on point. "No, the question is, what the hell are *you* doing?" I shot back. "I saw you with model bitch earlier today, holding hands and shit!"

The look of shock on Sam's face was priceless. She was actually surprised that I'd caught her! She walked over to the television set and shut it off.

"You got some nerve to be laid up in my house like you live here."

"Well, I came by your studio first to talk to you, and the baby-faced security guy told me you'd left for lunch."

Sam sucked her teeth at my mention of the security guy. "Damn it, it was that new dude! Everyone on staff knows not to let you in or give you my information."

"Whatever, Sam. Don't blame him for getting caught, though he did help. Anyway, I went to the restaurant to talk to you there and instead saw you all cuddled up with that bootleg Iman model. Is that who you were with last night? Because you sure as hell weren't here!"

"Wait, hold up... you were here last night, too?"

"Yes, and *you* weren't! Quit playing with me, Sam! You're my woman, and I'm not dealing with you laying your ass all around the city with every bitch that smiles your way."

"I'm *not* your fuckin' woman, Delilah. We went out a couple of times, and that was it!"

"That wasn't 'it,' " I corrected her. "That was the beginning of our relationship."

"You mean the beginning of your stalking! First you're blowing up my phone all the fuckin' time. The next thing I know you're popping up everywhere I go, making scenes in public, hollering about me cheating on you and sleeping around. I had to move my studio to a building with security just to stop you from harassing me at work and freaking out my clients, and you *still* show up!"

"What you call 'stalking,' Sam, is me showing you how much I care about you. I want us to grow as a couple, but we can't do that if I keep catching you messing around with other women like a bitch in heat."

"Grow as a couple? Damn, you really don't get it. We went out *twice*! I'm not cheating on you because I'm not in a relationship with you, Delilah. You'd stop 'catching' me with other women if you stopped stalking me. I can be with any woman I want."

I shook my head in disgust. "See, that's your problem right there, Sam. You're so damn cocky! Saying you can be with any woman you want, like you're fuckin' God's gift to pussy."

"God's gift? Woman, we didn't even sleep together! That's it, I'm putting an end to this bullshit right now." Sam pulled her phone from her coat pocket and started to dial. "That no-contact order from the judge means you're not supposed to be anywhere near me, Delilah, and breaking into my damn house is the last straw. I didn't want your ass to end up in jail, but if that's what it takes to knock some sense into you, then so be it."

"I got your little no-contact order from the sheriff. That doesn't mean shit to me, Sam."

"It'll mean plenty when the police get here!"

This was taking an unintended turn. If the fact that I did technically commit breaking and entering wasn't enough, Sam was right: I *was* violating the no-contact order she'd put in place against me. I'd tried to explain to the judge that Sam was just being vindictive, that I wasn't the crazy stalker woman she made me out to be, but he wasn't hearing any of it. And right now, there was no way I could get through to Sam and get her to call off the cops. Lucky for me, reinforcements had arrived. I spotted Lenore standing in the doorway, observing the scene.

"Thank God you're here!" I sidestepped Sam to get to Lenore. "Sam called the police. Help me talk some sense into her before they get here."

Lenore sighed and rolled her eyes at me. "You do know you broke into the woman's house, right? I told you to wait until I got here but you had to be all headstrong and do what you wanted. She had every right to call the police. You set your own self up."

"I know I was stupid. I'll admit that. But you're sensible. Sam will listen to you."

"Listen to who? Who the hell are you talking to?"

I turned around to see the confused look on Sam's face.

"I'm talking to my best friend, Lenore. She came to help me out with you."

"Help you out with me? Help you out how?" Seeing that I had back up must have spooked Sam. Her tone had mellowed and she spoke slowly, softly.

"Okay, Sam, I admit it. I shouldn't have come here and broken in. I apologize for that. Lenore told me to just wait in the car, but no, I had to prove a point and let you know that you couldn't keep messing around on me. But this wasn't the way to do it. So, she came over to help me talk to you."

Sam had backed away from me, her eyes wide in bewilderment. What was she so shocked about? Lenore was a tiny thing, made even more so by her constant apparel of oversized sweats.

She wasn't at all intimidating, so what was Sam shaken up for?

"Delilah…" Sam's voice was barely above a whisper. "There's no one here but us."

"What are you talking about?" I pointed to the doorway where Lenore was standing. "She's right there, clear as day." I looked at Lenore, who just shrugged her shoulders in confusion.

Sam's entire demeanor had changed with Lenore's arrival. "Okay, okay. I get it now, I really do."

I sighed in relief. We were finally getting somewhere with all of this.

Sam turned her gaze to the doorway, looking directly at where Lenore stood. "Um, Lenore, would you like to come in and have a seat?"

"Why is she talking to me like I'm remedial?" Lenore asked with a scoff. "You're the one acting a fool."

"Maybe she thinks we're going to jump her. Just sit down, and we'll sort this all out."

Before Lenore could move, a patrol car pulled into Sam's driveway. Seeing the authorities arrive, Sam bolted through the front door, nearly knocking Lenore over. I threw my coat on and ran after her. For all I knew she'd tell the police I was going to kill her or some other foolishness.

Two of Charlotte-Mecklenburg's finest, a man and a woman adorned in their police winter wear, had stepped out of the vehicle.

"Officers, look, this is all a misunderstanding," I said as I came out of the house. "There's nothing going on here, just a spat between lovers."

"Bullshit!" Sam said. "I'm not involved with this woman. She broke into my house and was waiting for me when I got here. I've got a no-contact order against her, and she's violating it. I can even get you the paperwork."

"Ma'am," the first officer addressed me as he walked forward. "Did you violate a judge's order?"

"I didn't do shit," I yelled, backing up. I wasn't foolish enough to fight a policeman, but I also wasn't going to let myself get manhandled like some drug dealer on *Cops*.

"You forget you broke into her house," Lenore offered from the doorway. "That's cause for arrest right there." I turned and gave her a nasty look.

"You're *not* helping, Lenore!"

"See!" Sam yelled at the police. "She's talking to someone who isn't even there!"

The officer nearest me glanced at the doorway, then looked back at me. His hand hovered above his cuffs. But surely *he* saw Lenore... right?

"Ma'am," he said again. "I'm going to ask you—and your friend—to come with us."

I looked at Sam, still standing next to the cop car. She looked truly terrified. The second officer was on the car radio, but I couldn't make out what she was saying. I glanced around the yard and realized a number of neighbors had come outside to watch the spectacle I was making. Here I was, just trying to have a sensible talk with my girlfriend, and it had avalanched into an embarrassing domestic situation on the front lawn with the cops. I was mortified.

"You gotta face the music, Delilah." I looked to my side. Lenore had come and stood beside me. Oddly enough, her movement had gotten no reaction from the police.

"You're right," I admitted with a sigh. I turned back to the officer. "I'll go."

The officer took the cuffs from his belt and placed them around my wrists. He led me to the patrol car with Lenore walking behind him. I guess since she didn't technically break any laws, she wasn't actually under arrest. I heard him recite my Miranda rights, but I didn't listen. My eyes were on Sam. She gazed back at me with an expression I recognized: a mix of astonishment, pity, and fear.

"It's okay," I assured her as I was lowered into the backseat. "We can still work this out. I forgive you for cheating on me, and I still love you."

Sam didn't respond. She turned toward the second officer and asked a question I couldn't hear.

"I'm not sure," the lady cop replied. "Situations like this have a lot of variables. She violated the no-contact order, but there are clearly some psychological issues at play here. She's delusional and hallucinatory… it's probably schizophrenia. That'll have to be dealt with first."

Hearing that, I sighed, closed my eyes and leaned back in the seat. I'd seriously fucked up, and the next few days were going to be hell because of it.

"You know where this is going, don't you?" Lenore's voice broke my thoughts. She was sitting next to me in the back of the patrol car, arms crossed and ankle over knee. "They're going to contact Dr. Harvell, and he's going to know you've been lying about me being around."

"I didn't have any choice," I defended. "If he knew you were here, I'd be back on those pills, and I hate the way I feel when I take them, like the world isn't real or something. Besides, having you around usually keeps me out of trouble."

Lenore scoffed. "And yet, here we are. All over some woman you can't let go of."

At that, I turned my head toward the window to get one last glimpse of Sam. She was standing in her doorway, watching the officers back away from her house and haul me off to God-knows-where—whatever place they took folks they called "crazy." But I knew better. The only thing crazy about me was my love for that woman. She didn't appreciate it now, but in time she would. I was sure of it. I believed that love *always* found a way. And as far as I was concerned, there was absolutely nothing crazy about that.

Erzulie's Touch
Claudia Moss

Bae-Girl sees the smiling woman first.

Near the sugar and flour aisle, around the corner from the small room where rows and rows of wine are shelved in the Farmer's Market. She seems to be posing. If she were a picture, Bae-Girl thinks, the caption would read "Paradise." Totally inappropriate for the rambunctious wind stalking the parking lot, her dress is thin and colorful with huge red, yellow and pink flowers. Bae-Girl guesses they are hibiscus blooms, the ones often shown in pictures of island resorts.

Right now the woman's large eyes follow Bae-Girl from the bins of squash and cucumbers to the glistening leaves of kale, turnip, collards and mustard. A bit uncomfortable under her gaze, Bae-Girl glances over at Norma Jean, who is chatting up an attractive mother of two— her usual MO— Bae-Girl has learned to accept whenever they shop at the market.

Bae-Girl shakes her head, locs heavy against her warm gray cardigan. She wipes sweat under her glasses. If Norma Jean had any sense, she'd quit that flirting and tell the chick to stop her baby from grabbing anything within her reach and make her toddler stop poking holes in plastic packages. Instead, Bae-Girl bags several ears of yellow and white corn and sneaks a peek over her right shoulder.

The woman's eyes yet smile. At her.

Quickly, Bae-Girl returns her attention to her wife, who is cooing at another young mother's giggling baby.

Goodness. A finger lasers her shopping list. Quietly, she resolves not to see the mysterious woman. So what if the woman stares until she leaves?

When she pushes the cart past Norma Jean, Bae-Girl reaches for a plastic bag posted on the end of a vegetable bin.

"*Hola, Querida. Veo que eres una mujer de calabaza, como yo. Si lo desea, puedo hacer un plato de calabaza asada que le encantará. Es delicioso. Mi madre es una mujer de calabaza, también.*"

Bae-Girl jumps, the words close, practically close enough to be in her head. She has to look up. Look over. The smiling woman is beside her, brown eyes intent on hers, teeth perfect. Whiffs of something sweet fill Bae-Girl's nose.

"Excuse me?" Bae-Girl puckers her brows. "I don't speak Spanish."

The stranger grins, selects a large, orange-yellow squash and presents it to Bae-Girl.

"*Lo prefiero con cebolla, ajo y nueces,*" the dark woman continues in a musical flourish. She winks, nudges Bae-Girl's arm. "Aquí. Pruébalo."

The way she places the squash atop the other vegetables in the cart sends Bae-Girl the clear understanding that this woman means to do something more than suggest she try a new dish. Her movements intimate, she takes over the shopping as if asked.

"Look, ma'am, you have me mistaken for someone else."

Bae-Girl speaks slowly, hard pressed not to notice the stranger's beauty. And instantly, it comes to her. The woman exudes the sweetness she smells.

"*Creo que necesitará tomates para servir con la calabaza.*"

Before Bae-Girl recognizes the word "*calabaza*" again, and equates it with the squash in her cart, the woman steps behind her, crossing the aisle to the Roma tomatoes. She drops three handfuls into a bag and plops the bag into the cart.

By the time Norma Jean shows up, the woman has pitched bags of cucumbers, potatoes and peas into the colorful cart.

"*Hola, amor,*" she greets Norma Jean. "*No te preocupes. Te encantará mi cocina también. Es un poco frío en este mercado.*"

Bae-Girl's gaze volleys from Norma Jean to the woman. Smiling, she remembers that her woman studied Spanish in college.

"Uh, honey, glad you could make it. This chick has taken a liking to me, so... what's she saying?" Her smile widens, a mischievous cast darkening her caramel eyes.

"Oh." Norma Jean's brows hike. "Really?"

Bae-Girl nods.

"*Hola, me llamo Norm y ella es mi esposa.*"

The woman scintillates, an orange hue beneath her skin set aglow. She bows. Her hand reaches for Norma Jean's.

"*Bueno, guapa. Con mucho gusto.*" In slow motion, she places her left hand over her heart. "*Me llamo Erzulie.*"

Pivoting, she offers Bae-Girl a handshake. "*Hola, esposa.*"

Bae-Girl smiles, impressed. "*Hola, Erzulie.*" Her hand is soft, kissably soft.

Norma Jean's forehead ripples. She reads the flirting, but the fluid streams of Spanish leave her speechless.

Bae-Girl crosses her arms as if to wipe away the attraction.

Erzulie never drops her smile, only hunches her shoulders and tilts her head.

"What was all the rest of that, Miss Interpreter?"

"Hell, if I know." Norma Jean laughs. "Something about the cold."

Bae-Girl mimics her wife's laughter. "Is that all you got, Sherlock?"

"If you can do better, carry on, e-spo-sa."

"Yeah, right." Bae-Girl turns to the already shopping again woman. She's now tossing bags of eggplant and spinach into the cart.

"Erzulie, where... are... your... people? We can take you to the information desk, if you like."

At that, Erzulie bows. Then continues shopping, saying nothing more to Bae-Girl or Norma Jean, until they arrive in the oblong shaped, checkout space.

"*Escucha, Bae-Chica y Norma. Voy a casa con ustedes dos. No hay nada más que decir al respecto.*"

That said, she pivots as if she already knows she, too, will be heading to their car in the next ten minutes.

At the register, Erzulie smiles and says, "*Hola,*" to a petite, brooding woman with a tiny red dot between her brows and then steps behind the couple. The groceries bagged, Norma Jean slides a card to pay the bill while Bae-Girl waits, perplexed, knowing the woman's dress, confidence and skin are the sole reasons she doesn't summon security.

...

The ride home oozes heat. By the time Norma Jean pulls into the drive, only then does she realize she has not touched the Jaguar's dash, although warmth and something that sounds like calypso linger in her thoughts and trail her into the solitude of the house.

No sooner than Bae-Girl and Erzulie face off in the kitchen, Norma Jean places the remainder of the groceries on the kitchen island and vanishes, leaving Bae-Girl to handle their impromptu houseguest.

"*Me encanta tu casa, Bae-Chica! Es grande*," Erzulie utters, covering her mouth, eyes saucer wide. "*Como muchas familias viven aquí.*"

Despite narrowing her eyes, readying her tongue to fire off the reckoning this chick deserves, Bae-Girl is an instant ice sculpture, melting inside, sliding and slipping. Confused.

Against her will, she understands Erzulie's childlike awe.

"Take a look around." She invites Erzulie to pass into the living room with a wave of her hand.

"*Gracias.*"

Bae-Girl's sole Spanish phrase is "*Por nada,*" which she says enthusiastically, watching Erzulie light up.

In the living room, soft sighs escape the smaller woman's finger-covered lips.

Any other time, Bae-Girl would have demanded another woman help put away the groceries. This time, she rinses and dries the vegetables alone. Somewhere between unpacking and ordering the refrigerator's shelves and bins, she wonders what has come over her. The night is crazy, she thinks, staring at the different types of squash. Before she could think one thought, she was feeling another, and both were conflicting... as though someone else was thinking for her.

Later, after she shows Erzulie to a guest bedroom, Bae-Girl joins Norma Jean in their bedroom to download momentarily before heading downstairs to prepare a quick dinner. On their white kingsize bed, she barely has time to enjoy her wife rubbing the weight of the day from her feet when the aroma of spices and singing summon her to the hall.

Electric outbursts of "*Azúcar!*" drift upstairs to the women from the kitchen.

"What's she saying?" Bae-Girl whispers to her wife, who hunches her shoulders dubiously.

"Not sure. I think maybe it's the word for sugar."

"Sugar? But she's singing, though. Just wrapped in laughter and sorrow."

Norma Jean nods. "I'm going down. Sounds interesting. I don't care what she's singing."

In the dining room, Bae-Girl and Norma Jean are dumbfounded. A piping hot casserole steams spicy beside a succulent green salad.

Norma Jean thinks she has transitioned without traversing the Valley of Shadows.

"*¿Tanto te gusta todo?*" Erzulie spreads her arms excitedly, proud of her culinary efforts. Her voice lowers. "*Lo veo en tus ojos.*"

Norma Jean remembers the words for "I like it" and shouts, "*ME GUSTA!*"

"*Bien.*" Erzulie nudges Bae-Girl. "*Que? ¿No te gusta calabaza?*" Her brows furrow. She points to a chair. "*Siéntate, encantadora.*"

Bae-Girl blinks.

Norma Jean only grins. "Hell, it's squash, I think."

Bae-Girl rolls her eyes and watches Norma Jean spoon mounds of a flavorful smelling food into a plate on the beautifully set table. She heaps a healthy serving of salad beside the savory dark orange delight, the salad dish unused.

Erzulie returns to the kitchen. Minutes later, another song serenades the amazed couple.

"Ask her what she's singing." Bae-Girl can hardly speak for the taste of sweet pumpkin laced with cinnamon and spices she doesn't recognize.

Norma Jean chews and shakes her head. "Don't care." Bae-Girl kicks her foot under the table.

When Erzulie switches songs for the third time, Bae-Girl quits chewing long enough to give Norma Jean a nasty look.

"Okay," Norma Jean says. "Damn." She swallows and calls

into the kitchen, "*¿Erzulie, uhuh...qué canción es esa?*"

" *'Rie y Llora.' Es mi cantante Celia. ¿Te gusta?*"

"Bae-Girl *gusta.*"

"*Gracias, Bae-Chica!*"

"Por nada!" Bae-Girl calls, none the wiser about the song.

Tickled, she returns to stuffing her mouth. "So what part of all that was the name of the song, Einstein?"

"Oh, sorry. The song's '*Rie y Llora,*' " Norma Jean explains between mouthfuls of sweet pumpkin casserole. "If I'm not mistaken, it means 'You Laugh and You Cry.' "

"And?"

"And what?"

Bae-Girl spears a dainty forkful of salad and shakes her head. "And what else? I assume she said more than the name of the song, correct?"

Norma Jean nods. "Ya know, I think she's Cuban. She said Celia was her singer."

"As in Celia Cruz?"

"You get the prize." Norma Jean laughs around a mouthful of salad.

Bae-Girl rolls her eyes, flat lining her lips. "I deserve it. Cruz made the song famous, according to a documentary I saw once. And get this, she and Maya Angelou were friends. Not only that, Maya became fluent in Spanish to be able to communicate better with Cruz and her other Spanish friends. Isn't that wow?"

...

For several days, Erzulie serves a combination of squash and salad so often Bae-Girl and Norma Jean become squash women, like Erzulie's mother. The vegetable shows up on the dining room table raw, sautéed, grilled, steamed, broiled, boiled, baked and fried. They never know quite how it will show up, alone or as a side dish. Erzulie adds it to rice pilaf. She cubes and grills it, sticking it daintily on long wooden skewers with other vegetables. She even plucks it in stews and serves the best pumpkin pie they have ever had.

After Erzulie has been with them for a week, a nightly goblet of wine shows up beside their plates.

Norma Jean appreciates the vibes that consume her every time she feels the spirit coursing through her body. It is, she tells Bae-Girl, as if an angel is reading her mind, manifesting her unspoken desires.

"That wine," Bae-Girl informs her, "means one damn thing. Trouble."

But Norma Jean is deaf under the red wine's good vibrations.

The following Friday they are lounging in the living room, exhausted from another harrowing workweek. And although Norma Jean has no complaints about her day job as the vice president of a large software corporation, the supervisory hours she puts in after her workday at Sweet Dreams, their yogurt shop, leave her drained.

Norma Jean brings a goblet to her lips and enjoys a grateful sip, most times holding it on her tongue before swallowing.

"Bae-Girl, what's up, love? What gives?"

"Look at you, Norma Jean. You know damn well what gives. She has gotta go. That's all to it."

Norma Jean sighs. Thinks about pouring more wine. If she had one more drink, she might feel her wife inside, like she used to.

"What would you be doing right now if Erzulie wasn't here? Somewhere cleaning and complaining, right?"

"Norm—"

"Answer the question, Bae-Chica." Norma Jean chuckles.

"See that right there is what I'm talking about. This is not a laughing matter. My father says strong drink and cards will topple a family as sure as shooting." She snarls at the goblet in Norma

Jean's right hand. "Look, wine costs money. Where is she getting the money to keep this house in nightly drink for three people? And don't think she's not hitting the bottle, too."

Norma Jean draws a deep breath.

"I haven't given her money. I don't know where she gets it, but I really don't mind."

The glass is cool against her lips, its liquid gently firing her insides. She feels her body relaxing into the embrace of the recliner.

"Okay, Norma Jean. So now you don't mind. Yesterday you didn't care. And right now you're drunk in gratitude. What's next?"

"Drunk in love?"

Bae-Girl longs to slap taste from her mouth. "Has it ever crossed your wine-pickled brain that we know nothing more about that woman than we did from the first day we saw her in the Farmer's Market? Did it ever cross your mind she might be illegal, hell, the woman doesn't even speak English for that matter, and that is strange. Even the Mexicans in my department at the State speak some English. We don't even hire folks at Sweet Dreams if they can't understand us. Damn, Norma Jean."

"*Cálmate, Bae-Chica.*" Norma Jean considers her wife as if she were a grumpy child. "*¿Qué es realmente el problema?*"

Bae-Girl glares sideways. She is not hearing this woman correctly. "How dare you tell me to calm down. And you damn well know what the problem is— you and her."

Norma Jean continues smiling, her gaze gentle on Bae-Girl's face.

"Would you kindly quit that damn smiling? I am beginning to think you are losing your ever-loving mind. Only crazy people do all that smiling."

"Crazy, gay and happy people, maybe?"

"I am not playing, Norma Jean."

"*Respirar,*" Norma Jean whispers. "*Sólo respirar.*" She reaches for Bae-Girl's hand on the arm of the sofa, but Bae-Girl jerks it away.

"Don't be telling me to breathe." Bae-Girl's mouth is taut. "You're going to heed your own advice when it goes down, and I know something is going down soon. I can feel it, sister. *Ahora tomaré.*"

Bae-Girl's eyes blink in confusion, as if she has just been hit with a bright beam. Where, she wonders, still blinking, did that last part come from? This is crazy. Was she going crazy? Because Norma Jean was already crazy.

At that moment, as if in answer to her query, Erzulie emerges into the room. She is wearing calm like perfume. As much as Bae-Girl hates to admit it, it is redolent and fresh, like the sound and smell of ocean breezes now filling the room.

"*Buenas noches, mis queridas pequeñas,*" Erzulie murmurs, glowing as if she is standing in spotlight. "*Me encanta verte disfrutar del vino. Un vaso una noche es ideal para tu salud. Es cierto, Bae-Chica.*"

Strangely, Bae-Girl nods. Despite her father's long-ago teaching, she has been feeling better with her one glass nightly, too. And on rare nights when Norma Jean works late at the yogurt shop, she enjoys wine alone.

Erzulie curtseys, bowing her head. Light brown coils halo her face. Her Spanish is musical when she says, "*Es un corazón saludable. Realmente.*"

She says the last part as if she already knows Bae-Girl will not believe that the drink will stave certain diseases, but she continues anyway.

"*Pero tu tienes razón en estar preocupado si se bebe más que el una copa. ¡Aumenta el colesterol bueno y diluye la sangre. Mi abuelita solía decir un vaso de vino al día mantiene a una mujer delgada y sexy.*"

Although the heart healthy stuff is good, too, Norma Jean really likes the part about Erzulie's grandmother saying a glass of wine a day keeps a woman thin and sexy. Yes, indeed, she thinks, looking over at Bae-Girl, who yet fixes Erzulie under a piercing stare. She ought to like that, too.

"*Me gusta,*" Norma Jean says, returning Erzulie's smile.

Inside, waves washing over her heart make her relax where the wine leaves off. In the white, rolling surf, she sees herself chasing a bikini-clad Bae-Girl down a sandy beach. Norma Jean enjoys the tantalizing thought of catching her. She sighs in gratitude.

"*Tengo una sorpresa para ti,*" Erzulie is now saying, swaying from right to left, her fingers a steeple.

Bae-Girl, whose concentration never leaves the woman's face, jabs her wife in the arm. "Pay attention," she growls through clenched teeth. "It's about to go down, like I said, but I just didn't think it would be this soon, so look alive."

Norma Jean play-frowns.

"*Mañana, el sábado, vamos a tener una fiesta.*" Erzulie's tone is exuberant. "*Será fabuloso y festivo. Y lo más importante.*" Here, she pauses and curtseys, before continuing. "*Esta fiesta es mi regalo para ti!*"

"*Gracias,*" Norma Jean says. "*Te doy las dulces gracias.*"

Erzulie bows and skips from the living room.

"What are you *gracias* about, Norma Jean? This woman acts like she is five, announcing she's throwing a gratitude party for us being her friends and all you can do is sit there talking about, 'I give you sweet thanks'? Are you crazy?

"Wait a damn minute. Hell, give me another glass of wine. I need it to wrap my mind around this charade."

Norma Jean gets up and pours Bae-Girl a fresh glass of wine. She brings it atop a napkin with "*Te amo*" embossed in ornate gold lettering.

"And where did this come from?" Bae-Girl's eyes point to the napkin saucily. "Thank you."

"*Por nada, mi angelita.* But about the napkin, I don't know."

"Right." Bae-Girl's eyes narrow.

"*Lo siento, Bae-Chica.*" Norma Jean does her best to fight a grin. "*Pero tú, mi amor, bueno ahora entiendo la lengua excepcional. Estoy muy orgulloso de ti.*"

Bae-Girl takes a sip of the wine. "Well, la-dee-dah. That is a part of the crazy around here that I am trying to get you to see. How in the hell am I understanding and sometimes speaking a language I've only heard for a few weeks? Don't you think something is wrong here?"

"*No sé, pero no.*" Norma Jean's tone is solemn.

In her head, though, Bae-Girl clearly hears, "Hush, please. If I hear Spanish one more time today, I will scream," but "*Silencio, por favor. Si he oído español una vez más hoy, gritaré*" leaves her lips.

...

Norma Jean's fist flies to her mouth.

As the first to arrive in the kitchen on Saturday for the evening's party, she looks at Erzulie and may as well have been a pillar of sea salt. What she admires could surely bring breath to the lifeless!

"*Buenas noches,*" Erzulie quips, naked except for red pumps and, for what Norma Jean could see, a red, white and black apron that strains to cover the front of the woman's shapely, soft-looking body. "*Estoy feliz de que verte.*"

"*Iiigualmente,*" Norma Jean stammers, smiling appreciatively. She couldn't help wondering if Bae-Girl would explode, though, like Morrison's Beloved, when she steps into their strip club of a kitchen. Bae-Girl could never be mistaken for a slouch, but this Erzulie is a piece of Lady Godiva chocolate to a desperate diabetic.

"*Cómo estás?*" Norma Jean asks, suddenly ecstatic.

"*Maravillo! Muchas gracias, amor!*"

Erzulie wraps her in a bold embrace that takes her breath and thoughts simultaneously. She emanates sunshine and blossoms, honey and daydreams. Norma Jean feels herself open. Feels her layers peel back, one by one, like she's never been exposed before. There is no rhythm, no rhyme. Not even a how.

When Erzulie's arms encircle Norma Jean's neck, soft coils tickle the underside of Norma Jean's chin and ripples her insides.

Even as she reflects on what could be keeping her wife, her arms encircle Erzulie's petite waist. The little woman feels good, Norma Jean thinks, so good, until she is damn near hyperventilating, something she once heard other women utter when they were lost in her arms. But thank goodness she doesn't allow her sweaty palms to weigh Erzulie's firm buttocks, for this woman's breasts pressing into Norma Jean's chest gradually synchronizes their heartbeats. Only then does Norma Jean realize just how long it has been since she and Bae-Girl made love. Minutes later, Bae-Girl practically slips up and topples across Norma Jean's lap at the breakfast nook in the kitchen.

"What is—?"

Norma Jean doesn't bother turning her head. She simply places a finger to her lips and shushes her annoyingly.

"*Hola, Bae-Chica! Estoy tan feliz de que estás aquí!*"

Bae-Girl rolls her eyes and frowns. "That's easy to see." She snorts when her wife signals for her to sit.

"Why is she in my kitchen na—?"

Norma Jean spreads her legs, leans in to her wife and whispers out the side of her mouth, "This is the party, honey. Don't be a pooper."

"Don't tell me what—"

"*Gracias a ustedes por ser maravillosa,*" Erzulie begins with brown-sugar eyes. "*Bienvenido a mi fiesta! En primer lugar vamos a preparar una comida y luego vamos a disfrutar de ella...aquí mismo en la cocina! Es bueno eso?*"

Bae-Girl can hardly believe what she is still seeing and hearing. "I am not eating anything prepared by a naked woman in my damn kitchen. Have you two lost your minds?"

"Awesome!" Norma Jean exclaims, straightening in her seat. "Great idea! What do you want us to do? And what's on the menu!"

"Shut up, please." Bae-Girl folds her arms angrily. "I'm not doing anything but throwing her out as soon as this party ends. Believe that!"

"*Sólo sentarse y disfrutar!*" Erzulie sings, lifting her arms as though she's on stage receiving applause.

When she pivots and washes her hands at the sink, her butt an up-side down heart, the top tapering off into the tiniest waist, Norma Jean and Bae-Girl don't know what to stare at first. That exquisite backside. Those sculpted thighs, thick and smooth. The shapely legs, oiled and sleek, in red pumps. A chewable handful at the bottom of her butt where ass meets thigh. The view is an Instagram moment.

From the refrigerator, Erzulie brings a large bowl of butternut, yellow, acorn, zucchini and turban squashes. There are luscious red Roma tomatoes, fresh garlic and purple onions. She gathers olive oil, coconut lemon pepper seasoning, chives and basil from the spice cabinet. Surveying the recipe's ingredients, she pops her fingers and strolls back to the fridge, where she bends, legs straight, and nearly disappears inside the cool space. The view is hypnotic. Under its spell, Bae-Girl's eyelids strike up a noticeable twitch. Rubbing is useless, though. It only withdraws and reappears in her bottom lip, encouraging her to stretch her neck to better appreciate the woman's cute honey pot. She resists and then she looks. Norma Jean, on the other hand, isn't resisting. Her attentive gaze studies every inch of the woman as she imagines what she'd like to do to her. Her body is motionless, on red alert.

"*¿Puedo sentarme en tu regazo para dados estos vegetales?*"

Bae-Girl nods slowly, amazed that she is about to do something she's never ever done before— allow another fem to sit on her lap. Pushing back from the table to permit Erzulie to better position herself atop her thighs while she dices vegetables, Bae-Girl runs her palms along the woman's luxurious thighs. She exhilarates in the heat pooling between her body and Erzulie's ass. Involuntarily, she inhales and begins a sensual grinding while gripping the small waist to maintain a firm connection. She can feel Erzulie tremble half way through the dicing, when her right thumb slides through dark pubic curls on its way to the woman's glistening rosebud. The gentle, circular motions cause it to swell and bloom. Erzulie has to lower her knife and ride the surf that Bae-Girl has created, not to cut herself.

Erzulie shudders when Bae-Girl lifts her warm cheek from her naked back and peers over at Norma Jean through an euphoric haze.

"*Es el regazo seco?*" she wants to know. "*Tal vez pueda terminar en dados los vegetales allí?*"

Norma Jean's head bobs excitedly. "Yeah. It's as dry as it can be right now. Feel free."

Her chair is already pushed back. When Erzulie sits and her weight sounds an urgent alarm throughout Norma Jean's body, she longs to lift the smaller woman, head to the sofa and throw her back out; however, she isn't calling the shots. She already knows Erzulie has been wooing Bae-Girl from the word Go, and she is a benefactor by default. But everything is everything. No complaints in her mouth.

On Norma Jean's lap, Erzulie continues dicing vegetables while grinding wet against Norma Jean's right pants leg. Her palms full of breasts, Norma Jean feels the world fall away, moist and urgent. Between her thumb and forefingers, Erzulie's party-hat nipples plump like raisins, lending the dicing a start-and-stop rhythm.

The onions are the last to be chopped.

At the sound of Erzulie's sensual moaning whenever she leans back toward Norma Jean's shoulders— sometimes half-standing and other times half-sitting, Bae-Girl takes the liberty of wiping onion tears from Erzulie's cheeks.

After all the ingredients are prepped and Norma Jean and Erzulie have shuddered through ecstasy, Erzulie takes her time standing and leans against the circular breakfast nook table. The stroke of two pairs of hands on her enflamed flesh stays her progress. Bae-Girl's touch is soft, silky, the squared nails gently skimming her hip and the inside of her right thigh. Then there is Norma Jean. Massaging, parting, incinerating. Once the heat dis-integrates enough for Erzulie to regain motion, she rinses squash and onions, spreading them in a large glass baking dish. She sprinkles three tablespoons of olive oil over the mixture, which is then seasoned with coconut lemon pepper seasoning and basil.

She pre-heats the oven to broil the veggies for 20 to 25 min-utes. While the oven heats, she rinses organic spinach and chunks the Roma tomatoes before tossing them into a bowl with the spinach and drizzles the salad with a threepart mixture of apple cider vinegar, honey and olive oil as a vinaigrette.

Into the fridge the salad goes; under the broiler the squash rests.

Inviting the two-some to stand, Erzulie smiles sweetly and places herself between them, standing, and begins a conscious-altering sway. Her Spanish comes in a whispertalk so low, the women do not bother with understanding. Simply, they follow the thrill of excavating nectar in dripping, finger-squeezing orifices.

Their moans and whimpers are lost in one another's raven-ous mouths. From Bae-Girl's hot tongue on Erzulie's left nipple and her hand fisting Erzulie's honeycomb to Norma Jean's teeth prints enticing the woman's tender sides and her palms imprinting a burgundy-red tapestry on her azz, the threesome is in paradise, sharing the same lips, fingertips, passion and release.

Much later, while the casserole cools and the salad chills,

Bae-Girl knows, now, just how she proposes to have Erzulie. One hand disappears under her, finding her pussy and her pleasure's pulse. She groans under Norma Jean's expert touch, her wife's hand anchoring her at the waist, her other hand attending to the fearful skin of her hipbone before it dips lower, one finger then others intoxicating the trail between her hips. With her body curled above Erzulie's, Bae-Girl eases her strap-on into a tight inferno and pauses. At her backdoor, Norma Jean pauses then enters, and together they light fireworks across Norma Jean and Bae-Girl's king-size, platform bed.

How could Bae-Girl have prepared for such a rush flowing like uncorked wine?

...

The following Monday, when Bae-Girl comes in from a long day, calling, "*Erzulie! ¿Dónde estás, querida? Me muero de hambre! ¿Qué es para la cena? Tengo mucho que decir! Erzulie!*" and Norma Jean calls to ask what Erzulie has prepared for dinner, Bae-Girl is the one to tell.

Over Saturday-night dinner at a friend's house.

They yet can't believe it, although Bae-Girl has told the story a thousand times from then to now. How she came in and the house was unusually quiet. Mausoleum quiet. No *calabaza* aromas. No warmth. No music. No singing.

Only empty wine bottles on the living room rack remind them that Erzulie ever was. Wine and their perspectives. At dinner, both circulate the table like a basket of warm, home-baked bread.

"Who ever heard of a Black woman around these parts not speaking English? That is just crazy is what it is."

"Did she take anything?"

"Wonder if she finally found her people?"

"Never thought I'd miss hearing Spanish."

"Did she ever wear anything other than sundresses?"

"You think she rooted us?"

"All I know for sure is we love *calabaza*. With everything!"

"We loved the place where three bodies know no beginning or ending. For real though."

...

Despite their running commentary, Bae-Girl and Norma Jean never forget Erzulie. They remember her in the sudden re-blossoming of their love for one another. An intense attraction had drawn them together when they met and quickly led to them falling in love and later exchanging marriage vows. But since Erzulie's arrival, the women begin making love as if for the first time. Each touch is gentle, explorative. Their lips are softer. Sweeter. And definitely more passionate. To her surprise, Bae-Girl finds herself speaking Spanish whenever she strokes Norma Jean's back at the end of a tedious workday, something she once did unasked. Likewise, Norma Jean becomes mindful. Of small things. Like giving foot massages, preparing calabaza dishes, bringing Bae-Girl impromptu flowers and, best of all, running the rose-petal baths Bae-Girl loves. In secret, Bae-Girl is the one who broaches the subject of inviting another lover into their relationship. Erzulie had opened her and Norma Jean in unimaginable ways. They never envisioned themselves dating another woman, as a couple. Yet here they were, smiling into other women's eyes, those who intrigued them, mentally and physically. Nowadays, whenever Bae-Girl and Norma Jean caress in long, heated embraces, in mind-blowing foreplay and memorable lovemaking, they think of Erzulie and the unexpected beauty of another's touch in one's life.

The Cigar Box
Sheree L. Greer

I

The house sagged. The porch seemed to bow under the weight of history. The windows, dusty and dull, reflected the soul of the house, heavy, forbidding, and lifeless. Iris rang the bell. She hadn't been back to the house since the day her father died. She rang the bell a second time. She glanced over her shoulder and out onto the street. Cherry Street was quiet, empty. Winter in Wisconsin always silenced the streets. The cold chased people into their homes and the snow held them captive. She rang the bell a third time. She wouldn't ring it again. When her sister Beulah called and pleaded with her to come over to the house, Iris's first inclination was to say "no." She hadn't spoken with her older sister in over five years. The call surprised her almost as much as Beulah's tone– apologetic, humble, insistent.

Iris peered into the window closest to the front door. She couldn't see inside. Just as she turned to head down the split and cracked wooden steps, the door opened.

"Little Iris," Beulah said, "you came." She held open the screen door with one hand and held her sweater closed with the other. She didn't smile, but her face softened at the sight of her sister.

Once inside the house, Iris followed Beulah into the kitchen. She sat down at the table, and Beulah poured them both a cup of hot tea.

"I'm glad you decided to come, Little Iris," Beulah said. She took a seat across from her sister.

"Well, you said you needed to talk about something important." Iris shrugged.

Beulah nodded. "I'm selling the house."

"Okay."

The two women sipped their tea in silence. Iris didn't have anything to say. She had no investment in the house. She didn't want anything, wasn't interested in any remnants or keepsakes— all reminders of the lies and loss that framed their family.

"Just okay?"

"Yes," Iris said. "Sell it. Good. Fine."

"Since it's just us, I suppose we could split the money we get for it. Whatever it is."

Iris drank her tea. "I don't even know if I want any money from it."

"Don't be stupid, Iris. Of course you want some of the money. You and Arthur and those children."

"We're fine."

"Still proud as ever, I see." Beulah held her cup with both hands.

"It ain't about being proud, Beulah," Iris said. "And the only one being stupid is you. I can't believe you're so oblivious to what went on here."

"What the hell are you talking about?"

"Daddy, Beulah. Your beloved Daddy. What he did to Christine. Don't act like…"

"Shut your mouth right now, Iris." Beulah slammed her hand on the table.

"No. I won't. You know. You probably knew all along."

Beulah stood up. "I won't let you sit here and talk ill about our father– our dead father!"

"Oh, I remember," Iris smiled, her eyes cold as the howling winter wind.

"You're sick, Iris. How can you sit there and talk bad about Daddy? How can you make up these things about him? These things about Christine?"

"I'm not making it up!" She felt like a child again. When she and Beulah were little, they argued all the time. If Iris said water was wet, Beulah would argue the opposite, a million different reasons Lake Michigan and the Sahara were one and the same.

"If something happened, and I'm saying *if* something happened, how would you even know? Huh, Iris, how would you know? You were out in the streets the second you could make it to the end of the block without tripping. And I won't even mention how you high-tailed it out of here right after you finished school. Ran off with a man like you didn't have no life of your own. Leaving Christine in the garage and leaving me to—"

"That's what this is about? Me leaving." Iris shook her head. "Do what you want with the house. I don't even know why you called me about it." Iris stood up. She buttoned her sweater and grabbed her gloves out of the chair to her right.

"This isn't the way this was supposed to go," Beulah said. "We're sisters, Little Iris. We're all we got."

Iris looked at her sister. Dark circles framed her eyes and deep creases lined the corners of her mouth. Beulah looked older than her forty-two years, more tired, more slouched and weak. Iris thought back to Christine's letters. When Iris left with Arthur, Beulah hadn't fared too well in life. She'd taken up with Arthur's cousin Gooney, who turned out to be a womanizing drunk who couldn't stay in one place too long. Beulah gotten pregnant by him, but she lost the baby. Christine wrote that the miscarriage took more out of her than anything else. Iris supposed Beulah started looking after their father, Louis, as a distraction, someone who needed her like her baby would have, someone that needed care and attention. She suddenly felt sorry for Beulah. She looked away from her sister and focused on her cup of tea, lest Beulah see the pity there and resent her even more.

"Beulah," Iris started then stopped. "I don't know what to say."

"You don't have to say anything," Beulah said. "Don't leave yet. There is something here that you'll want."

"I've told you. I don't want anything from this house…"

"Please."

Beulah left the kitchen. Iris contemplated leaving, but picked up her tea instead. She took one last sip and placed the cup on the table. When Beulah returned, she held a cigar box in her arms.

Tears burned the corners of Iris's eyes. She held her hands out to receive the box. Beulah placed it carefully in her younger sister's hands and stepped back, watching Iris blink back tears and marvel at the box.

Christine's cigar box. The wooden box smelled of smoke and tobacco. Iris sat down and set the box on the table. Sliding open the top, Iris looked over at Beulah, who had retreated to the doorway as if the box might explode. She sneezed. Dust tickled her nose and stung her eyes. She dug around in the box. Rolling papers, a Zippo lighter, a couple flints, dried tobacco leaves and flower petals, and a few coins slid around the wooden bottom of the box as she poked around. A slip of paper with Iris's Buckettville address scrawled in Christine's slanted cursive sat atop a small roll of unused stamps.

"Where did you find this?" Iris asked. Her voice crept out, buckling under the intense grief the box summoned. She held the box up to her nose. She inspected it further, noticing charred corners and chipped paint along the top and sides.

"It was in the garage," Beulah said. "I found it when I went through the remains of the fire. Christine had a small chest. It was open and overturned when I found it, lots of ash and burned paper all around it. I think they were your letters."

Iris began to cry.

"I found the box underneath the chest." Beulah took careful steps toward her sister. She placed a tentative hand on her shoulder. "It's the only thing left of her, Little Iris. And I think you should have it."

The younger sister collapsed onto the box, her sobs taking over, her shoulders shaking as she cried. Beulah squeezed her sister's shoulder and when Iris turned toward her, she embraced her. Iris wrapped her arms around her older sister and wailed. Beulah rubbed her back and bent over, pressing her lips against Iris's hair.

"I'm sorry, Little Iris," Beulah said. "I'm sorry for everything."

Beulah put on more tea and the two sisters talked about the house and how best to proceed with the sale. Iris was still adamant about not wanting any of the house money. Beulah insisted; Iris relented. Beulah brewed more tea, and the two sisters sipped Orange Pekoe and talked well into the evening, sharing stories and catching up on the last few years of their stand-off. Iris, not entirely detached, had sent her sister a blank holiday card with a family portrait inside. Beulah mentioned how beautiful the children were and told Iris about her miscarriage. For the first time in many years, the two women talked like friends, smiled and shared like sisters. At random intervals, the conversation thinned and Iris would run her fingers along the edge of the cigar box until either she or Beulah broke the silence with another story.

Before Iris headed home, she drove her car around to the alley behind the house. She pulled up alongside the space where the garage had been and sat staring at the open space. She looked over at Christine's cigar box, which sat in the seat beside her, a passenger, almost like Christine rode with her. She returned her gaze to the empty slab of concrete where the garage used to stand. A knock on the passenger side window made her jump.

It was Red.

Iris reached over and rolled down the window. Cold air instantly blasted into the car.

"Long time no see," Red said. She smiled. Red, a close friend of Christine's, had only recently moved to Milwaukee. Having spent only a couple weeks each summer with her mother and the rest of her time down south with her father, Red wasn't around enough to forge any lasting relationship with Beulah, Iris, and Christine while growing up. Red and Christine's friendship came as a surprise to Beulah and Iris, who both regarded Red as "that girl" for most of their lives.

"Indeed," Iris answered.

"I'm here checking in on my mother." Red wore a heavy wool coat, fuzzy white hat, and thick white scarf, but no gloves. She cupped her hands over her mouth and blew into them. "Didn't think I'd run into you though."

"I don't really come over this way. Soon I won't have any reason to come over this way at all."

"What you mean?"

"Me and Beulah are selling the house," Iris said. She wasn't sure why she was giving Red any information. Something about her eyes made her want to talk. Iris glanced down at the box. Christine had written that very thing in one of her letters, that Red made her want to talk, want to open up.

"I see. Guess there's no reason to keep it if neither one of you are going to live in it," Red said. "I was sorry to hear about your father."

Iris bit her bottom lip.

"Your sister didn't care for him much. She had more than enough reasons. But, she never cursed him or wished him ill."

"Christine was special like that," Iris said. She wondered

how much Red knew about her family, how much Christine had shared with her.

"Yes. Yes she was." Red stood up straight and hid her face from Iris's view. When she crouched back down, her eyes were wet with tears. She wiped them. "Guess I'll see you around." Her mouth strained into a smile. She looked down at the cigar box and the smile eased into something natural, authentic. "Take care, Iris," she said.

"Red, wait," Iris said. "Come by my house tomorrow. I've got something for you."

Red raised an eyebrow. She nodded her head. "Sure."

Iris gave Red her address. When she pulled off, she looked into her rearview mirror and noticed Red walking into the center of the cement slab where the garage had been. She sat down on the cold, snow-dusted ground and crossed her legs beneath her. By the way her body shook, Iris knew that Red was crying for Christine.

Red arrived at Iris's house exactly when she said she would. The clock in the front room chimed three o'clock and before the last note of the whimsical tone, there were three knocks on the door.

"Red," Iris said when she opened the door, "come on in." She took Red's coat and hung it on the rack near the door. She motioned for her to take a seat on the sofa.

Red sat down and looked around the living room. The boldness and energy of the colorful room struck her—orange and yellow pillows on the tweed furniture, red shag carpeting with gold flecks, which were highlighted by the shimmering golden clock hanging above the television set. There were pictures of peacocks with rainbow tails flared defiantly, orange tigers with black lines slashed across their faces and muscular bodies, and landscapes of African grassland, giraffes and bushwillow trees against glowing sunsets of crimson, violet, and burnt umber.

"Would you like some coffee?" Iris asked.

"If you're having some," Red said. "Have you ever been?"

"Been where?"

"To Africa." Red pointed at the painting.

"No," Iris said. "Not yet." She stared at the painting. She had fallen in love with the picture the moment she saw it. She bought it from the Carpet Man, a brother who parked his black van in parking lots and spread large area rugs across the hood and side of the vehicle. One day, he had paintings and pictures leaning against the side of the van's sliding door. Iris set her sights on the picture of Africa and transported herself halfway across the world. She longed for the real thing, for the wonders of the world. "Have you been to Africa?"

"No," Red answered. "It's on my list though." She chuckled to herself.

"What?"

"Just my list keeps getting longer and longer. Even with all the traveling I do."

"Where have you been?"

"Oh, here and there. About every state on the East Coast and all over the South. I've been to Europe– Paris, Barcelona, and Rome anyhow. Spent some time in Haiti and Jamaica." Red squinted and twisted her lips, as if she struggled to remember. "Bermuda and Hawaii. Yeah. That's it."

Iris smiled. "You've been to all those places?"

"I just end up places sometimes," she said with a shrug.

Iris shook her head in disbelief. She wanted to say something. "I've been to Buckettville, Alabama" she could counter. She felt inferior. She looked at her guest, expecting her to look away, but she didn't. Red smiled a gentle, humble smile at her. Iris realized she was being silly; it wasn't a contest. Red hadn't even asked her about her own travels, and it wasn't in a rude, self-centered way, it was gracious, as if she didn't want to put her on the spot or embarrass her with what was clear– that she hadn't been anywhere, that a picture of Africa was as close as she would get for a while.

Iris returned the smile and excused herself to get the coffee. Before she pushed open the swinging door to the kitchen, Red called out after her.

"Don't misunderstand, Iris," she said, frowning. "All travel ain't vacation."

Iris returned with a tray of coffee and shortbread cookies. Red took her coffee black with sugar, and Iris added cream to her coffee until it looked like liquid caramel and tasted just as sweet.

"So, Red," Iris started, "I know you and my sister were very close." She stirred her coffee, watching it swirl.

"We were."

"She wrote about you, but she didn't get a chance to tell me everything. She wrote that you… you were her very best friend. She said that she had told you things and that she was ready to tell me things." The tears came. They weren't welcome, but Iris didn't fight them. Red put a hand on her knee. Iris cleared her throat before she continued. "Did she… did she tell you what she wanted to tell me?" Her lips trembled, and her eyes pleaded. "Did she tell you anything that you think I should know? I want to know everything. I need to know everything."

Red bit at her bottom lip. "Your sister and I talked a lot. She told me many things. Some of them were obviously painful for her. But if she didn't write about it, then…" she looked Iris in the eye. "I just don't feel right telling you what she told me in confidence. I promised her that her secrets, her joys and her pains, were safe with me." Red swallowed against her own tears, her voice starting to waver. "Though she's journeyed on, I have to keep my word. I've got to keep my promise to her."

Iris exhaled loudly, frustrated and disappointed. She stood up and sighed again. "I understand," she forced out. The words barely audible. "I'll be right back."

She went into her bedroom and into the closet. On the top shelf, next to a wide-brimmed hat and a small collection of hand-bags, sat a white shoebox tied closed with a red string. She pulled it down and returned to her guest.

"I want to give this to you." Iris handed the box to Red. "I'm not sure why. It just feels like the right thing to do."

Red set her coffee down and took the box from Iris. She untied the string, lifted the top of the box, and gasped.

Inside, the box held one of Christine's nightgowns, the one Iris had held on to for years, clean and neatly folded.

Iris watched Red as she stared into the box. She lifted a hand and pressed her palm against the fabric. She rubbed its softness, fingered the lace eyelets, then lifted the nightdress out of the box. As the bottom of the nightgown unfolded, both Iris and Red held their breath.

A blood stain, dulled but ever present, cried out.

Iris looked away.

Red could not.

Iris turned at the sound of Red's muffled sobs. Red held the nightgown against her face and cried into it. Iris watched her. A complicated knot of emotions tightening in her chest.

Jealousy gripped Iris. Christine had told Red about Louis. Christine had shared things with Red that she hadn't shared with her. Christine had loved Red, and Red had loved her back. Iris didn't doubt how much Christine missed her while she was away, her letters were clear– she was loved and missed, but Red had done something Iris couldn't do. She had gotten Christine to open up. With Red, Christine found a purpose, a reason for love, an excitement for life. All the things Iris had wanted so badly for her sister, wanted so much to help her find, were found with this other person, this other woman that was not family, that was not a sister, that was not her.

Red pulled the thin fabric from her face slowly. She cleared her throat and carefully re-folded the nightgown, placing it gently in the shoebox.

"Thank you," she said.

"You're welcome," Iris said. She took a deep breath. Red covered the box and re-tied the string. Iris placed a hand on Red's shoulder. "Can I ask you one thing?"

"You can ask," Red said with a small smile.

"You and Christine," Iris said. She paused. "Were you two… Did you two… Were you…"

Red grinned and looked down at the box. She raised her eyes to Iris.

"It's like I said, Iris." Red tightened the knot she had made in the string. "If Christine didn't tell you…"

Iris rolled her eyes.

"I'll tell you this. I loved Christine very much. And though she never got around to saying so, I know that she loved me, too." Red rested her hands on the box with a soft thud of finality.

Not the answer Iris was looking for, but it would apparently have to do. Iris smiled and rubbed her hands on her slacks. Red stood up, box in hand, and glanced one last time at the picture of Africa on the adjacent wall.

"I should go," she said.

Iris rose from the sofa. The two women faced each other, love for Christine a bond between them. Red set the box down abruptly and pulled Iris into a tight embrace. They held each other, eyes closed, hearts beating in time with one another. Neither of them heard the door open, but they both jumped when it slammed shut.

"Who the fuck is she?" Arthur said. The smell of whiskey and cigarette smoke filling the room as he stumbled forward.

"I'm Red. Ruby, really." She smiled. She picked up the shoebox and walked around the cocktail table. She extended her hand toward Iris's husband.

Arthur looked at Red's hand then looked at his wife. "Where's the kids?"

"They're out with Viola and her girls." Iris sighed. "Why are you being rude, Arthur? This is Red, a friend of Christine's."

Arthur narrowed his eyes and took Red in from head to toe. "I didn't think Christine had any friends," he said.

"Arthur, you're drunk. Just take your ass in the room and lie down," Iris said.

"I don't want to 'lie down.' Kids gone. You got company. Shit, maybe I should get like you. Invite some people over. Entertain." He scoffed in Red's direction and wiped his mouth. His lips wet and loose, his speech was slurred, but had bite all the same.

"Red, you should go," Iris said. She lightly touched her arm and urged her toward the door.

"She ain't got to leave," Arthur said. He made his way toward the kitchen. He stopped in the middle of the dining room, patting his pockets, looking for his cigarettes. "She can stay. You ain't content running the streets with your friends, you gotta bring 'em home, too?" He slid a Pall Mall between his lips and lit it. It dangled as he spoke, "You make time for these bitches, but can't make time for your husband. For your kids." He pulled out a seat and plopped into it. He sat with his legs spread wide, his arm thrown across the back of the wooden dining room chair. He took a long pull of his cigarette and shot the smoke out of his nostrils.

"What the fuck is you looking at? I can't party with y'all? No dicks allowed?"

"Arthur, hush all that noise! Take your drunk ass to sleep!" Iris yelled.

"Iris," Red lowered her voice as she spoke, "I don't know if I should leave you here with him like that."

"Like that? Who the fuck you think you talking about? You think I can't hear you talking about me?" Arthur stood up.

Embarrassed, Iris grabbed Red's arm and moved her closer to the door. She removed Red's coat from the rack and handed it to her. She took the box from her as she adjusted her coat and put on her hat. Iris handed the box back to Red and opened the door. She didn't put on her coat, but stepped outside with Red anyway. The winter air felt good against her face, which had gone hot with rage and humiliation.

"I'm sorry. He's drunk and talking stupid." Iris crossed her arms, holding herself against the crisp, arctic air.

"How often is he like that?" Red asked.

Iris smacked her teeth and looked past Red. She watched a car, slowly driving up the street, gray clumps of snow falling from the wheel wells.

"How often?"

"It doesn't matter, Red," Iris said. "It's fine."

Red placed a warm hand on Iris's arm. "Does he hit you?"

Iris's eyes bucked at the question. She took her bottom lip between her teeth and looked up the street again.

"Iris, does he hit you?"

"No," Iris lied.

Red tightened her lips. She gently squeezed Iris's arm. Her eyes searched Iris's for the truth. Iris knew what she was looking for, so she looked away.

"Look, you don't know me. You don't know my life. Everything's fine," Iris said.

"It's like I told you before, Little Iris." Red grabbed Iris's face, forcing her to meet her eyes. "I loved Christine, and in my love for her, I love you, too. I'm your sister, too."

Iris moved her face away. Even with what they had shared, Iris didn't feel entirely comfortable with Red using the name Christine gave her.

"Thank you, but it's okay, Red. Don't worry." Iris took a step backwards, rubbing her hands up and down her arms. The January chill had reached her bones, it reached deep, gaining strength from the stress and emotion of the afternoon. Suddenly, she ached all over, from the inside out.

"I'm going to go get in my car, but I'm not going to leave until you give me the okay. You go upstairs and see about that man. If he tries anything, anything at all, you come on out, and I'll take you somewhere safe."

Iris shook her head. "Good-bye, Ruby Red. You take care of yourself."

"I'm not leaving until…"

"Good-bye, Red." Iris turned, running up the few steps of the porch and disappeared into the house.

…

When Iris entered the house, Arthur had dozed off in the chair. She cleaned up the cocktail table, placing the coffee cups back onto the tray as quietly as possible. She crept past Arthur carefully, but not cautiously enough. He grabbed her arm, his hand like a vice-grip. She froze. Her husband looked up at her with the cold of winter in his eyes.

"Arthur, let go," Iris said, her voice shaky with exhaustion and anger. "I said, let me go."

Arthur grunted and shoved her away from him. Iris stumbled toward the window, the cups and coffee condiments teetering. Reaching out to steady herself against the window pane, the tray tipped and everything on it crashed to the floor. Iris regained her balance and raised a hand toward Arthur. He caught her by the wrist, squeezing and twisting her arm as he stood up.

"I heard about that bulldagger you been partying with," Arthur said. He pulled Iris's arm up behind her back then pushed her into the window. The cold glass numbed her face. Dirt and a thin layer of ice covered the outside of the window.

"What?"

"Don't lie to me," he whispered into Iris's ear. "That what you into now?"

"She's a friend, Arthur. Just a damn friend."

"I got your friend," Arthur said. He pressed her into the window, still yanking her arm up, her hand almost touching her shoulder blade. "Fuck with me if you want to, Iris." He let go of her arm and pushed her head into the window. Her forehead bumped the glass. Later, the spot would knot up and wouldn't go down for almost two weeks.

Iris cried. She lifted her arms and grabbed at her husband's shirt as he walked away from her. He twisted out of her grasp. He turned before pushing through the kitchen door.

"Clean all that shit up," he said.

Although Iris hadn't done anything wrong, she felt guilty. Before cleaning up the cracked coffee cups, shattered saucer, and scattered cookies, Iris walked over to the front door. She opened it. Red's Buick LeSabre, clean and silver with exhaust billowing out the tailpipe, sat idling across the street. Red had wiped a circle into the foggy driver-side window, and although Iris couldn't see her face, she knew her sister's friend looked up at her with concern and curiosity. She had looked at women that way before, women she worked with, women she saw on the street, women who smiled and waved, who whispered to themselves that everything was fine.

Iris raised her hand and waved down at Red. She forced her cheeks to rise, her lips curling into a pained smile. She waved and nodded, whispering against the window that everything was just fine.

Red called twice a day, but Iris didn't answer. The phone would ring three to five times, once in the morning and once in the evening; the calls going unanswered each time. When the phone rang in the evenings and Arthur was home, both he and Iris would look at the phone then at each other until it stopped, the staring contest like a dare. He dared her to move, she dared him to say something. Without really noticing, the two had called a truce of sorts. Both of them coming home and staying home in the evenings after work. Dinner with the children and getting them tucked in for bed. Quiet time with Arthur in his chair and Iris on the couch. He read the paper, she flipped through magazines. A couple weeks and Red got the hint. The calls stopped, and the silence in the front room became deafening.

The husband and wife lay in bed, back to back, the only noise in the house the dripping faucet echoing down the short hall that lead to the bathroom and the children's rooms.

"Arthur, what are we doing?" Iris said into the darkness.

"What you mean?" Arthur said. Neither one of them moved.

"What are we doing? Is this… is this all there is?" Iris blinked and swallowed slowly, waiting. She wanted an answer. A grunt. A sigh. An arm to come wrapping around her body and stubbly chin on her shoulder.

The bed creaked as Arthur turned onto his back. Iris took a deep breath. In one quick, resolute movement, Arthur swung his legs off the side of the bed and pushed himself up. He paused, popping his neck, and left the room.

Unfinished Business
Ashley Sullivan

Leah had been driving for ten and a half hours, with only a fifteen-minute break to gas up, get lunch, and use the restroom. She loved this trip down South, and made it as many times a year as she could. She loved to see the way the landscape changed from flat cornfields in Indiana to rolling hills in Kentucky, and craggy mountaintops in Tennessee. Then, finally, the sharp green pines and luscious kudzu in Georgia. Sometimes, she'd take 285-W and go around Atlanta because it was less traffic, but most times, she just stayed on I-75/85-S and drove straight through the heart of downtown. Atlanta was one of her favorite cities in the U.S., and as soon as she hit the I-20 bottleneck she'd turn on the radio and get crunk for the last hour of her trip. She generally listened to podcasts the whole trip down; they kept her alert much more so than the music on her iPod, which always made her sleepy. Leah turned the radio to V-103 to see what new songs were hot; she had no idea since in her small Midwestern town, there were no R&B radio stations. Another reason she needed to get the hell away from that place.

After another hour of driving, she arrived at her destination.

As usual, her parents were happy to see her. Dad had cooked her favorite meal: steak and baked potatoes on the grill, a nice green salad, and plenty of crusty garlic bread. It was predictable, but that was one of the things she loved about coming home, time seemed to stand still. Leah seemed to be the only person who'd changed: her hair had more salt than pepper these days, and she'd even lost a little weight. She was looking good, but she hoped that wouldn't be too much of a distraction when she met with Alexandra the next day. Alex was always one to turn on the charm, showering her with compliments and making her feel like the most beautiful woman in the world. For this and other reasons, Leah could not afford to lose sight of her goal tomorrow. She had to tell Alexandra that it was over, for good.

Leah and Alex had been fooling around for years. It had started when they were both seeing other people. They knew it was wrong, and didn't give a damn. Back then, both of their girlfriends had been too self-absorbed to notice the too-long glances, the hugs that lasted just a beat too long, or the way that Alexandra and Leah always seemed to end up in the same place at the same time. Honestly, it was easy enough to do, the circle of lesbians in their town was small, and they always hung out together. Everyone was close, but no one knew just how close Alexandra and Leah had become.

Still, Leah was amazed that they'd never gotten caught. Carla, her girlfriend when she met Alex, had been in the closet and didn't much care what Alex did as long as no one thought *she* was gay. Hell, everyone but Carla knew that Carla was gay, and at some point, Leah got tired of dealing with Carla's internalized homophobia. That was no excuse for cheating on her, but it certainly made it easier to do it. Early in their relationship Leah had argued with her about never going out, Carla's lack of attention, and their non-existent sex life. Carla had been indifferent. By the time Leah met Alex, she had been frustrated and lonely.

Ironically enough, Alex and Leah had met at an anniversary party. Whose party escaped her, it had been so long ago. But Leah remembered how struck she had been by Alexandra that night. She was gorgeous: smooth cocoa skin, tall and muscular, with a cute short haircut that showed off a sexy neck. She was dressed in the style of the day: white T-shirt neatly tucked into her faded jeans, a crisp white Ralph Lauren button down oxford over the undershirt, and her loafers and belt matched perfectly. Small gold hoop earrings added just enough softness to her tomboy look. Leah remembered wiping her mouth with the napkin she had been holding, because she knew she was drooling and it wouldn't do for her to walk around smelling like spit the rest of the night.

Leah forced herself out of her reverie and spent the rest of the night catching up with her family and watching a little television. She arose early the next morning, did a little writing, and graded a few papers.

"Even when I'm on vacation, I'm working," she thought to herself. "Welp. All work and no play buys Leah a new BMW." Just then her cell phone rang.

"Hello."

"Hey, sexy," replied the soft voice on the other end of the phone.

Leah's breath caught in her throat, but she was able to keep her composure. She hadn't recognized the phone number, but she hadn't forgotten the sound of that voice.

"What's up?" Leah was trying to play it cool, but the sound of Alexandra's voice sent a deep shiver down her spine, and a tinkle to her lady parts.

"You. When you coming to see me?" Leah knew that Alex expected her to come to her hotel room, where they might engage in certain carnal activities. Except Leah had other plans: she'd see Alex all right, but she was determined to be rid of her for real this time. They had gotten too old for this mess, and to be honest, she was over it. Yes, Alex was still as sexy as ever, and yes, they still had a lot of chemistry. It was all that they had, and Leah was ready for more, only she didn't want that with Alex. She cared deeply about Alex, but she'd never trust her enough to be in a real relationship with her, Leah knew her too well. Alex was a liar through and through, and would never be faithful to any woman; the past five years had been proof of that.

"Well, what about dinner at La Croix tomorrow night? We can talk there."

"OK, sexy, does seven work for you? I'll pick you up."

"No thanks," Leah replied. "I'll meet you there. See you tomorrow." Leah hung up quickly before she had a chance to respond. Alex thought she was slick. Leah knew if she picked her up she'd be stuck with her until Alex was ready for her to go, and Leah wasn't having that at all.

...

While getting ready for dinner the next night, Leah reflected on the past five years, particularly the times that she had spent with Alex. After she had broken things off with Carla, Leah had been single for a while. She busied herself with graduate school and then work, having landed a tenure track job at a good university before she graduated. It was a long way from home, but that was how she liked it; she refused to be closeted by the rampant homophobia in her small, southern hometown. Alex had run off and joined the Air Force, leaving a trail of broken hearts in her wake. They'd kept in touch, and somehow managed to see each other quite often, regardless of where they were living. It was a lot of fun at first, planning rendezvous in different cities and sneaking around their hometown so no one would see them. They weren't afraid of being found out; more often than not, Alex hadn't told her family she was in town and didn't want them to see her. They'd shared a lot of good memories, mostly great sex and laughing at past indiscretions.

At one point, they even tossed around the idea of settling down into a "real" relationship. Leah nixed that idea when she found out that Alex had a girlfriend in Hawaii, where she had been stationed at the time. She was surprised that Alex had lied to her about the other woman; up until that point, they'd always shared information about whom they were dating or sleeping with at the time. Hell, she'd even met some of Alex's "friends." In retrospect, Leah realized that it was ridiculous, Alex was a liar, and even though Leah had made a point to be honest with her over the years, it seemed that Alex would never be able to do the same thing. It was a long time before they saw each other again after that. Hawaii had been a turning point in their relationship; Leah realized that things needed to change, although they continued to see each other intermittently for the next year or so.

Leah shook her head to clear it of the memories and return her mind to the present. It was time to get this break-up party started. She checked her lipstick and make-up in mirror, waved good-bye to her parents and walked out of the door. She drove the fifteen minutes through town to get to La Croix, her hometown's nicest restaurant, but decided to wait in the car since she was a little early. Leah hated to be late for anything, and she hated to be kept waiting. On more than one occasion she'd left a date when the woman hadn't shown up on time. She had a fifteen minute rule: If you didn't show up or call within fifteen minutes of the scheduled meeting time, she was out of there, no questions asked, and no second dates either.

After about five minutes, she heard the telltale booming of Alex's SUV. Alex liked her music loud, although you'd think that at damn near 40 years old, she'd have outgrown the impetus to show up everywhere with a booming bass.

Leah checked her lipstick one more time, and opened her car

door. Alex had already spotted her car and made her way over to her. She immediately grabbed Leah up in a bear hug and refused to put her down.

"Girl, if you don't put me down I'm going to scream!" Leah was joking but she really did want Alex to put her down.

"I'm sorry baby, I'm just so excited to see you. You're looking good enough to eat." Alex had a soft southern drawl that sent shivers down Leah's spine every time she heard it. Tonight was no different, but she had resolved to be strong.

Alex looked amazing as usual, although she had let her hair go natural and was now wearing locs. It looked good, but Leah liked it better short. "Oh well," she chuckled to herself, "this might be easier than I thought."

"Come on, let's go inside. Let's have a drink at the bar and then decide what to do after we chat."

"Bet."

The bar was dark and quiet, the perfect place to have this conversation. After ordering their drinks, they made small talk for a few minutes. As they chatted, Alex pulled her barstool closer to Leah's and put her hand on Leah's thigh. They had always been very affectionate, even in public, but tonight, Leah removed her hand as quickly as Leah had placed it there. Alex looked at her in surprise.

"What's wrong, baby?"

Leah decided this was as good a time as any to get to the reason for this meeting. "Nothing, but there is something that we need to talk about."

"Okay." Alex never did have much to say, probably because most of what she did say was a lie.

"Well, you know that I care about you."

Alex stopped her before she could finish her thought. "Wait a minute, are you trying to cut me off?"

Leah was a bit taken aback by Alex's question. She had

counted on the element of surprise helping her out with this. The last time they'd met, Alex said that they'd never stop seeing each other, and the audacity of that comment had haunted her for some time. It was also one of the reasons she knew she had to let this go. She now realized that it was probably a way to keep Leah off guard. She'd probably felt that this was coming back then.

"To be honest with you Alex, yes. I'm ready for us to stop. I'm tired of playing with you. It's over between us. I'll always have a special place in my heart for you, but this meeting up and going at it like jackrabbits is finished. We'll never be anything more than sex partners, and that's not the future I envision for myself."

"Don't tell me you're still mad about Hawaii! I told you I was sorry and I broke it off with that skeezer a long time ago." Alex had raised her voice and Leah was starting to wonder if she had been drinking before the date. The last time they "took a break" she had barely batted an eyebrow when Leah told her that she didn't want to see her for a while. Leah sat back on her stool and shifted her body so that she was now a little bit further away from Alex. She also picked up her keys off of the bar and held them tightly, just in case she had to make a quick exit. Once before, they had been in an argument and Alex had taken her keys. That night, instead of breaking it off Leah had ended up in Alex's bed, and she refused to let that happen tonight.

Alex's military-trained eye caught her movements and she immediately became contrite.

"I'm sorry, baby. I didn't mean to yell. I'm just upset. I can't believe you don't want to see me anymore. We can be together for real now. That's what you want isn't it? To have me to yourself?" Alex softened her voice and Leah was reminded of her ability to sweet talk women when things were getting dicey.

Leah allowed her body to relax a little, but she held on to her keys. "No, I don't want you to myself. I don't want you at all. Come on, how long did you think this was going to go on? This is never going to work out and hell, you have a girlfriend right now! What about her? Wait a minute, I don't even know why I'm asking you that, I know it doesn't matter to you. But it matters to me."

"It never mattered to you before."

"You know what, Alex? It did matter. But I was stupid and selfish. And you know what else? I've grown the fuck up. I'm better than this, even if you aren't. I don't need a fuck buddy anymore. I don't need *this* anymore."

"So you are just going to throw away all of our history? Don't you care about all the moments we've shared? Don't you know that I love you?" Alex's eyes were filling with tears, but Leah had seen that before. Leah knew that Alex could cry on command and was thus unmoved.

"You might love me, hell, I believe that you probably do. But the only history we have is that we started this so-called relationship by cheating on our girlfriends. The only thing we shared was our ability to lie with a straight face to the people we claimed we loved."

"Who is she?"

"What do you mean, who is she?" Leah was a bit perplexed. She had been single for the past two years and Alex knew that.

"Just what I said. Who is she? There must be somebody else."

"Seriously, Alex?" Leah was getting angrier by the minute, but she refused to lose her cool in public. "You claim to know me so well, so you must know that when I say there's nobody else, that's exactly what I mean. And just to be clear, there doesn't need to be another woman in my life for me to want to stop fucking around with you. Like I said, I've grown up. I'm not like you. I don't have to lie to get my way. I don't have to lie about seeing another woman, because I don't have a reason to. And I surely don't have to lie about why I want to leave you alone."

"Well, I'm not going to stop seeing you."

"Girl, you must be drunk. You live three thousand miles away from me, gonna be pretty hard for you to see me without my permission."

"I've surprised you before. You can't stop me from coming to see you."

"If you want to keep getting that nice military officer's pay I can. Don't play with me, Alex." Leah knew that she'd never call Alex's CO, but Alex didn't know that. Alex loved her career in the military, and as trifling as she was in other areas of her life, she'd never do anything to tarnish her career.

"You wouldn't dare!"

"Try me." Alex stared at Leah like she'd never seen her before, and Leah held her gaze.

Alex sat back on her barstool with a sigh of defeat. "You really mean it don't you? It's really over between us, isn't it?"

"Yep."

"You know what? I knew this was coming, but I didn't know how to stop it. I really do love you, Leah, but I know that I can never be the woman you need me to be."

"It's OK, Alex. It really is. We've had our fun, but it's time to be grown-ups. It's *been* time. I'm not mad at you, I never could be. I started this mess with you, but now it's time for me to finish it. I was hurting and lonely when we met, but that wasn't a reason to do what I did, even though Carla never found out about us. How many women have you lied to, Alex? You probably don't even know. Is that how you want to go through the rest of your life? I don't. I'd rather be by myself. I've made a choice to be a better person, to never repeat the sins of my past. You can do the same thing, you know."

Alex took a sip of her drink and chuckled softly. "Nah, I'm not ready for that just yet." Alex leaned toward her and Leah caught a whiff of her cologne, Chanel Bleu, one of her favorites.

"One more time for old time's sake?" Alex gave her a sly smile.

Leah hesitated for a moment, as if trying to decide. She took a sip of her drink and slowly got up from the bar. She picked up her purse, threw a twenty-dollar bill on the table for their drinks, then leaned over and kissed Alex lightly on her cheek. She whispered one word in her ear:

"No."

Leah turned around and walked out of the bar, and she kept walking until she reached her car. She pushed the ignition button and exhaled a sigh of relief. Until then, she hadn't even realized that she had been holding her breath.

Eshrei
Lauren Cherelle

Mother Allaida invades my mind as I rinse Rosalyn's hair. She comes to me, even when I'm away. "Daelo," she says, "a good Mother monitors her flock." I twist my neck to lessen the tickle of her breath.

Mother Allaida calls me *Daelo* because my life force is ripest during menstruation. For four days each month, I travel north to endure the pain of my thinning womb with Mother Allaida. The aches unlock *mae-vi*, which is the clarity I need to read a year into our Mothers' future. On the fifth day, I'm released to leisure and regain my physical and mental composure.

Troi's *mae-vi*, among her other gifts, was more mature than mine. On any given day, she could sit on the floor, using the stiff surface to swiftly balance her mind and spirit. Then, she closed her eyes to submerge herself into the last half of our Mothers' past and the next quarter of their existence. In the depth of transference, she smelled and tasted pieces of her visions. On a harvest moon, she could transport my *mae-vi* with her own.

When Troi passed away, Mother Allaida lost her prophet. That makes me a prized possession among her collection of weaponry.

Yet, I find no consolation in serving the Dynasty any longer. What good is clairvoyance when I can't see my own destiny? *Mae-vi* didn't help me save Troi, the only woman I've ever adored.

I'm retained in Mother Allaida's chambers four days each month, cloaked in silk and pampered like a Sister. But, I am no Sister. I acquired *mae-vi* from Troi. The gift is a side effect of her love, one that she trained me to access. Before *mae-vi*, I was simply a maiden of the Lourde Dynasty, a circle of Mothers who rule and protect the southeast region. Years ago, Supreme Mothers claimed this land to fortify a safe-zone for people of the diaspora after New World Order failed. The collapse of single currency led to global disorder and the beginning of World War IV. A decade of bio and tech warfare crushed society and nearly exterminated our brethren.

Supreme Mothers, who were forsaken in the old world, found salvation in the pit of humanity. For years, the gifts of their life force were suppressed by sociopolitical and patriarchal supremacy, suffering a society they did not create. Upon witnessing the old world's last breath, they claimed the land between the fallen cities. They fed and nurtured their people to form communes of peace and purpose, and fortified the communities with remnants of solar technologies to sustain what little resources survived warfare and near desolation. Their efforts introduced a new generation to freedom, a privilege Supreme Mothers hadn't truly experienced. Their children bore a lineage of Sisters with a fragment of the gifts our Ancestors held in the Motherland.

These gifts, however, were not conjured by their freedom. Their abilities were a reward from Ancestors for Supreme Mothers' strength. It took many, many centuries for Supreme Mothers to retrieve their throne. But they survived every second of exile.

I brush aside the countless stories Mother Allaida stuffs in my head. She loves to speak of days past. She believes that upon her passing, she will live in our hearts and stories as a Supreme.

Troi warned me what would become of her, though I will never tell Mother Allaida that she's mistaken. She is built with fragile esteem and absorbed with those beyond our land who only care for her trade. These vices sickened The Mothers in the old world. Mother Allaida will meet her demise, but Troi never told me when.

In six days, I journey for five hours to the core of our empire to rest with Mother Allaida and assume my role as Daelo. For now, I'm Sadiqa.

I wrap Rosalyn's shoulders with a towel and raise her wet head out of the sink. Rosalyn grips the towel at her throat to catch beads of water dangling from her coiled tips. I cover her conditioned hair with a gold cap and pat her arm.

Rosalyn rises and follows me to the dryer. She relaxes in the squishy seat, ready to let the heated air massage her shoulders and lull her to sleep.

I turn to Keva, who patiently waits for me to return while tapping her heels to a mellow harmony. She thumbs through one of the old-world magazines I've scavenged from the ruins.

"So?" I pump the salon chair three times to lift Keva. "What fancies you this week?"

Keva catches my gaze in the mirror. "These women didn't appreciate what they had." She thumps the scratched magazine page, a spectacle of two women with flawless brown skin, bright smiles, and false pleasure. This magazine, like the others our Supreme Mothers coveted, is filled with spectacles for companies they never owned.

"I want to reflect Mother Allaida," Keva says. "She is so beautiful. She never unravels her crown."

"If my neck was adorned in colorful diamonds every day, my hair would never travel past my ears. You and I have nothing to flaunt except skin. Bless Mother Allaida, but she doesn't have your freedom."

Keva smiles. "You are right. I am not a Child of the Dynasty.

ESHREI

I will not mimic royalty this week. Puffy is right with me."

I grab a metal-toothed comb to section her hair, coating her charcoal strands with a moisturizing mist before twisting a bouncy plait. Row-by-row, I cover Keva's head in thick plaits. When I reach the last quarter, I catch the shuffle of footsteps at the front door. The shop door opens, ushering damp, woodsy air inside.

"I'm into the night, friend. You can be my first day." I wait a moment for a response from the walk-in, but only silence meets my ears. I release Keva's hair and turn to my entrance.

I blink several times to erase the threatening vision before me. But my effort fails. I still see Troi in the doorway. Troi squints as if she can't identify the figures before her. This time, I drop the comb and rub my eyes. The contact spears my forehead with pain as my mind rushes to fully register Troi's condition. I wouldn't react this harshly to an apparition. Troi has found me.

I inhale deeply as her energy reaches me. Her shallow breaths impede her senses. Stuffy air bombards her face as she takes a narrow step into the shop. The dizzying music toys with her unsteady footing. Severe smells of hair products and electric heat settle in her stomach. Her life force is constrained by her injured body. I'm overwhelmed by her agony.

Duty calls, but I can't move. If I were still a maiden I would be severely punished for not steering Troi to a resting place. Mother Allaida would cast me to the ruins for six days to suffer the torment of lost spirits while starving and shivering. On the seventh day, she would shave my head and toss my dead locks into the courtyard. Then she would flaunt my shame for all to witness and pity.

These dreadful thoughts, however, don't unbind my feet. When Troi falls to her knees, Keva leaps from her seat. She's trembling too much to stay still, and much too afraid to look in Troi's direction again. Keva breaks the snap at the nape of her neck, letting the protective drape descend to the floor as she rushes across the room for Rosalyn.

She lifts the dryer hood from Rosalyn's head and shakes her awake. Rosalyn's eyes slide open with confusion.

"Track home, my friend."

"Why?" Rosalyn asks. She feels her hair for damp patches until her eyes find Troi. Her heart sinks, weighed down by the sight of a Sister in distress. She springs to her feet to help Troi but Keva pulls her away.

"Let them be."

Keva grabs Rosalyn's bag from the dryer seat and leads her into the rain, leaving both their shawls on the brackets at the entrance.

"Sadiqa," Troi whispers.

Her pleading tone helps me to see past my anxiety. A Sister, especially one I love, has never asked for anything. A Sister doesn't ask; only desires. Doesn't wait; only receives.

Tears consume my face. "Have I met my last day?" I selfishly ask. This measure of defiance would be matched with death in Mother Allaida's chambers. "You died."

Troi falls forward, her hands slapping the wooden floor. "Even now," she says weakly, "Allaida's lies fill your head." The pinch of cracked ribs constricts her breath. "I'm…" The effort stings, but Troi forces the words. "Not here to kill you." She swallows, the tang of today's blood as strong as yesterday's.

Relief softens my stance and I reach for Troi's hand. I lift her onto her feet and guide her to my chair. Troi slumps in the chair, waiting for the pain in her lower back to subside. I step away and watch as she collects a long breath for the strength to sit straight. "Shave my hair."

I freeze again, caught between her command and our customs. I shouldn't disobey a Sister a second longer, but can't will myself to commit an offense.

Our eyes meet in the mirror. "My heart is still with you."

I sigh, comforted by her affirmation. I'm pleased that my past and present betrayals are forgiven. I move a little closer to Troi. She has always carried a halo of soft, sensual energy that was difficult to ignore or escape. To every other maiden, Troi was distant and steely, and much too loyal to Mother Allaida to fancy other women. I, however, felt safe in her presence, allowing her force to seduce my curiosities. The memories and the gentleness of Troi's voice make it safe to stand by her side. She's exhausted and smells of banishment. The stains in her damp clothes are as visible as the crud in her matted locs.

Troi bows her head and I grab clippers. I position the teeth at the base of her head and graze her scalp, pausing every few seconds to let patches of entangled hair fall to my feet. I clip her wooly hair to a thin, jet-black layer before carefully trimming her hairline.

When I sweep the mess of hair off her shoulders, she opens her eyes and feels the roundness of her skull. Then she closes her eyes to share her thoughts with me. Her closeness quiets the grief I've carried for a year. She touches the bone above her right eye, bone crushed in the surge of Mother Allaida's fury. She awoke in the bush, an expanse beyond the ruins, a territory where Supreme Mothers once resided.

She roamed barefoot and alone for months among brush and the dust of human remains, her body healing too slowly from malnourishment and loss.

"Show me," I say. I need to know why she was taken from me.

"No, that existence is over. I live for Troi today."

I still want a glimpse of her history, but won't overlook her present needs. "Stand, Sister. You should wash."

I lead Troi out the rear door and along the concrete path to my home behind the shop. I light my throne of candles to illuminate our faces, saving my reserve of solar power for the shop. Troi stands in the center of my home, just between my kitchenette and bed. The room is airy and comfortable, but the confined square space feels strange to her.

I sit on the bed, giving her space to acclimate to the surroundings. "You have needs. Speak."

Troi turns from the dining table to me. Her body is starting to feel normal again. I feel her rising warmth, but the pang of hunger won't subside. Her presence strengthens my *mae-vi*, granting me insight into her last meal. She has only eaten once during her five-day journey. She stopped at a small café off the red road near the mouth of the empire for something she could keep in her stomach. She expected to dine-in until stares of disavowal pushed her onto the street. Some were surprised that Troi was alive. Others didn't care whether she was dead or living. To them, she was a traitor who should have remained an outcast, letting her spirit perish and body wither away. Their thoughts were hostile, but they wouldn't dare challenge her beyond hardened looks.

Troi appreciates my welcoming eyes, but she doesn't seek devotion of her maiden. "Fear drives your concern," she says and enters the washroom.

I approach the door and rest my hand on the handle. I can't separate myself from her, even for a second. I close my eyes to join her. She examines herself in the mirror. Without hair, her face feels abandoned, which makes her entire body seem bare. The feeling is healing. She enjoys the lightness and the separation from Mother Allaida's authority. When she lifts the hem of her shirt, I twist the handle to lend my help.

"No!" she says. "Go away from me."

She pauses at her chest to relieve the tension on her distressed muscles and waits for me to retreat from her head.

Obediently, I step away from the door. Though I won't stop listening. Her feet meet the bathtub before she opens the spigot and unleashes a stream of water. The soft flow caresses her bruised skin. A hushed moan escapes her lips.

ESHREI

I listen to the water falling from Troi's firm curves. The smooth stream incites my longing. I close my eyes and pleasure my thoughts with her body. My hands dance up her stomach and rest on strong arms. I touch my nose, recalling how herbal incense coats her hair. I bite my lip to lessen the warmth of skin on my face. I miss the comfort of her weight and her sheltering spirit, and the moments she stole from Mother Allaida to rest with me. When she wasn't traveling beyond our land to protect Mother Allaida during trade, she resided with me.

I walk to the pantry and search through my inventory of food. I can't rewrite the past or stitch the gash of my failed allegiance, but I will do anything to foster Troi's restoration. First, she must heal and feed her life force. I know how much she enjoys sweet and savory dishes with flavors that explode on her tongue. I grab a tray of spices and my freshest meat, along with bread and two pomegranates.

I split the fruit, spilling crimson seeds as lush as my memories. I busy my hands with the meal, leaving my thoughts free to cruise to Troi's soft places; places such as her lips and the doorway of her fortress. I imagine her inside of me as my hips rise from the bed, her thrusts separating my body from my head. The floating sensation invokes an orgasmic energy that only Troi can release from me. Her toffee eyes are as mesmerizing as the sultry words she whispers on my lips. I step away from the stove and touch my chest, my skin flush from cravings of food and flesh.

The washroom door opens and I return to the counter. I plate our food, paying close attention to Troi's approaching steps. She stops behind me, her eyes stroking my skin. Her hesitation worries me. I'm unsure whether I should move or speak.

Finally, she moves. Her arms enclose my waist, causing me to melt in the vibrations of her life force. Her hands flow to my hips. "There was a time when I drank your words," Troi whispers. Her lips graze my ear. "The taste has escaped my mouth but never my memory."

I face the lover I converted to an enemy. "I betrayed you," I admit. I press my bosom into Troi, leaving a slither of space between our lips. I need her kiss of forgiveness.

"I'm here for Eshrei. Later, I deal with you." She lets me go and takes her plate. "Where are you?"

I drop my head with remorse. A year ago, when Troi confronted Mother Allaida, I couldn't find myself. I dreaded the aftermath, so I sided with cowardice. I should have suffered the consequence of loving her, even in the rise of dethronement. My passivity caused me to lose Troi and abandon Eshrei, her only child. Now, I fight my tears, sparked from regret and the anger that arises from her stern question. She has the gift of sight, but won't use it now to seek answers. She only asks to carve a divide she doesn't want to cross with me.

I sit at the table and tie my emotions enough to speak. "My cycle renews in six days."

"When you go, don't speak of me."

"Mother Allaida will know. She will smell the happiness you stir in me. There is no way I can keep you from my thoughts."

Trio slides her plate away and pierces me with irritation. "You choose to remain a leaf without a tree. Find a branch and keep it."

She leaves me to rest where she feels most comfortable. For the next six days, she heals in the rising sun and sleeps under the eye of the moon.

. . .

Troi watches me in the dark morning as I lay in bed. I stall, basking in the quiet morning and her soft breaths. I'm unprepared for what lies ahead, unprepared for my spirit to assume life as *Daelo*.

"Sadiqa," Troi says, commanding me to wake.

I roll to my back and seek her face.

"Is Eshrei within the gates?"

"I've lost her," I confess. I stand with merciful eyes. "I can find her. Please? Please trust I can do this. I will never turn from you again."

Troi sighs, an expression of emotion she rarely emits. She steps away from me, conflicted by affection and disdain.

"Please," I say. "Don't let stubbornness stand between us. You came to me for a reason."

I reach out and touch her back, longing for more of the words she breathed in my ear last week.

Troi walks to the doorway. "Until your return."

"Yes." I smile, my heart infused with her sprouting trust. "Until I return."

. . .

When I arrive home, I find Troi in the shop fidgeting with my supplies. I sit by the door to subdue fatigue while watching her smell shampoos and conditioners, elixirs made by sea women.

"Why do this?" she asks. "We can tend to our own hair. What of this old-world custom fixates you? Our Supremes labored for money."

"My services are free, love."

She sets a hand dryer aside and looks to me for the answer I did not give.

I stand on aching feet and approach her. "I travel two paths, which makes it difficult to traverse in this village. The sea women are welcoming. But from there, the journey to Mother Allaida is too lengthy. The shop is how a maiden with privilege makes friends."

"And what has become of this maiden's last journey?"

I drop my eyes. Though I'm saddened by my news, I'm happy that Troi asks rather stealing answers from me. For the last four days, I had to lay with Mother Allaida, exposing my nude body so she could fully access my *mae-vi*. I'm thankful that Troi spares me of another invading touch.

"Mother Allaida didn't leave my thoughts or my side. I couldn't call for Eshrei without risking your return. It took every inch of my being to keep you out of her view. But, I *know* that Eshrei does not reside within the gates."

Troi closes her eyes, distressed that her *mae-vi* won't locate her daughter. Mother Allaida's cocoon is impenetrable.

"Go and rest," she says, her eyes directing me to my house. "At first light, we go to Ruthie."

"Ruthie? She gives direction that you must follow or else she curses your gift. She is selfish. She serves her own needs."

"Seems the two of you once had something in common. Rest."

I awake just after dawn to find Troi stuffing a bag for our four-hour walk to the forest in search of Ruthie. I watch her in silence. It's strange to see her work for someone other than Mother Allaida.

My evening of rest helped restore a portion of my energy. Troi takes breaks along our journey for my benefit. She stands by my side and hands me water and sweets. When we reach the last stretch, Troi spreads a mat on the forest floor. We sit together. I nibble on bread while she traces Ruthie. The old woman often shifts the land to conceal her dwelling.

"She's ridiculous," I say. "Only a woman with enemies would have to disturb the land for protection."

"Hush."

I pipe down so Troi can piece together Ruthie's movements. Her heartbeat slows as her *mae-vi* elevates. I feel warmer as it expands. The forest is silenced at the height of her vision. Her deep breathing replaces the tuneful birds and rushes of wind.

Without hesitation, Troi leads us to Ruthie's refuge, concealed in the slope of a rocky valley. Troi stops short of a narrow wooden door and waits for Ruthie to answer. When the door swings open Troi advances, though no one is in sight. I follow her footsteps with trepidation about this encounter.

"Aye yi yi!" I hear as the old woman appears from the shadows. She raises a finger to my face. "You should be grateful I let you cross my threshold. Keep your feet at the door."

Ruthie moves to the stove, dragging her right foot along. She seems tiny against the low ceiling. She wobbles with a pot of steaming water and two cups to a small round table. She sits in my direction. "You think I'm hiding?" she says to me. "I've retreated to this valley because this vision of mine is failing me." Ruthie squints and tilts a lantern toward her tea. "Rest with me, Sister."

Troi leaves my side to sit at her left.

"In my day," the old woman says, "a maiden was more than flesh. She wasn't born for servitude. She was a compass, here to steer The Mothers' direction toward the will of our Ancestors. I don't need sight to recognize what you are. A common whore."

Troi immediately raises her hand. Any response is unacceptable. I bite my tongue as my heartbeat surges.

Ruthie releases a teasing laugh, her abundant waist wiggling with amusement under her dress. She dismisses my company and coughs her laughter away. Quietness fills the quaint, square room as Ruthie drops tea bags in the cups. "She comes?"

"For truth," Troi requests.

"Blessings, daughter."

Ruthie pours water into her guest's cup before filling her own. She passes the cup to Troi. After Troi takes her second sip, Ruthie tastes her own. Now, she can speak. "She comes?"

"For," Trio says, her voice cracking under the weight of an aching heart. "For Eshrei."

"I am a book of tales. Some true, some false. Whatever the case, my words come with a cost."

I cross my arms to force myself from reacting to the old

woman's flippant reception. Her delay is unnecessary.

"What do you want from me?" Troi asks.

"Allaida's head."

"That's a charge unknown to this Dynasty. The Mothers would convene."

"My sister, you knew this day would come. Now you have to decide whether your daughter is worth Allaida's head?"

Troi looks at me as if I can grant permission on behalf of our people to commit such a transgression. I want to speak. I want to beg Ruthie to reconsider, but I can't jeopardize Troi's search for direction.

"With Allaida gone," Ruthie says, "you have nothing to fear. The Mothers will absolve you."

"I no longer have a place among their ranks."

"You made a mistake when you confronted Allaida a year ago. You should have asked the Mothers to convene and avenge their wayward sister. Instead, you sought to destroy a sickness without a cure. You were rash. But, they know your flaws."

"And yet, they didn't come to my aid."

"Only because you were foolish. You knew that Allaida had plans to seize northern territory, and that her trade was a guise to map its resources and leadership. The Mothers are content with peace. Nevertheless, Allaida is drunk with power and you helped her drink. You fought her battles and cherished the scars. That is until she favored your daughter. Allaida wounded and banished you and then boasted of your death to assuage her weak ego. The Mothers allowed you to suffer because your life force won't befall an untimely death."

"I've had a year to come to those conclusions."

"And so I arrive at the truth you seek. You are tall and strong and filled with the endurance of our Supremes. You planted a seed in your womb to honor womankind and sustain the Dynasty. Eshrei *is* a gift, a precious gift that merited her mother's protection. Instead, you let maidens tend to your child, which has allowed Allaida to trap a power that was born from your own. Eshrei has entered womanhood in her twelfth year. Her gift has matured and made her a slave to Allaida."

Troi's eyes glaze over as she places the cup on the edge of the table, barely meeting its surface.

"You're embarrassed by your ignorance," Ruthie states. "As you should be. No woman or man possesses the transport we need to cross the oceans and connect in spirit *and* presence with our people."

Ruthie takes a slow sip. She breaks her swallow and squints at me like I've spoiled the taste in her mouth. "Look away!" she says with a wave of her arm.

Gradually, I release my breath and avert my gaze to the floor.

"Sister," Ruthie continues, "this has been our home and refuge for nearly three centuries. Your child ushers a second wave of freedom our Mothers have prayed for relentlessly. Eshrei is a vehicle this world has never known.

"There is a white sand island within sight of the western bay. Take the sea boy's ferry and then travel by foot to a pair of cottages beyond the hills. In three days, return with my payment. Will go right nicely with my collection. Go to Eshrei and let her show you the glory of her gift. She will bring you here."

Our daylong journey to the west beach raises the hair on my neck. We keep to the old-world paths, once hardened with asphalt. The way is flat and lonely. We encounter no strangers, enemies, or friends. The puffy clouds are gracious in our efforts. They follow closely, sheltering us from the jarring sun. Even the wind generously kisses our skin. The easy travel scares me of what lies ahead.

Troi keeps quiet most of the way. She only stops for me to eat and regain strength. Each time, I eat quietly and approach her thoughts. And each time, her heart is heavy with guilt.

"Eshrei has always loved you," I remind her.

Troi nods. She reaches for my hand and helps me to my feet. We walk into the night, until we meet the sea boy's territory. The village of men builds boats from walnut and rope. They're slow to speak to arrivals. Most stare from their doorways. Only four boys approach us with lanterns. They stand side by side with bare chests and outstretched hands. I place dried mango in their palms. We wait until the tallest one comes forward and leads us to a boat. He skillfully guides the vessel across the dark choppy waves to the island at the foot of the mainland.

"Hmm," he grunts before I hop off the boat.

I reach in my sash and give him a handful of mango chips.

We cross the sand and pause at the brush. Troi listens to the trees for traces of her daughter's pulse. We rest for a few hours until dawn nears. Then we move cautiously as Troi tracks each step that Eshrei has taken.

At last, we reach a grove that shades two white cottages. We wait behind a mossy red cedar and listen for inhabitants.

"Eshrei is on the right."

"And Allaida is with her," I add.

Troi studies me. "No Mother?"

"I'm free of that addiction."

Troi kneels before a smooth large rock to direct her senses. She drops her hand near her foot and removes a blade the length of her boot. She grips the gold encrusted handle and positions the blade on the rock. She drags the blade from heel to tip over and over again. The press of metal against mineral excites me.

The seventh time, I move forward to stop her hand. I am ready to proceed. And this time, I will not fail.

One More
La Toya Hankins

"*One more* bite honey and then you can leave the table," Toni's mother said to the petulant six-year-old staring with hate-filled eyes at her plate.

"Do I have to? I ate all my lima beans," Toni whined to her mother.

"Yes, you do. I worked hard in that kitchen to fix you and this family a decent dinner. The least you can do is finish it. Be a big girl and eat your food," Alice McDonald said to her youngest child. Outside the window, the dusk of the October night stood in contrast to the light over the dinner table.

"But Mommy I'm full," Toni said, willing her features to look like another bite would take her over the line.

"You are not full until I tell you that you are full. Now stop complaining and clean your plate. Everyone at this table is finished but you. Even Octavia ate all her food and yet there you sit."

Casting an eye downward, Toni registered the absence of food on her best friend's plate. Usually her fellow second grader didn't join her for dinner during the week. However, Toni's mother had offered to let her stay the night to allow Octavia's mother to work late. Picking up her fork, Toni attempted to corner that last piece of hamburger stuffed pepper to put in her mouth but the task seemed too much. She dropped her fork on the plate making a subtle clatter.

"Toni Imani McDonald, I know you're not clanging silverware. Now finish your dinner so everyone can get up from this table. If you don't, then I'm going to take your friend home and she won't be able to spend the night."

Shaken by the thought of Octavia leaving her side, Toni inhaled the last portion to the eye-rolled appreciation of her twin 13-year-old siblings.

"Thank you, baby. Octavia and you can go. Hurston and Hughes, the two of you can clear the table," her mother said.

"Ma, that's not fair," Hurston complained while her brother got up and began removing plates. "Toni needs to clear the table. It's her turn and she is the reason it took so long for us to finish. I'm supposed to call Patricia in about ten minutes to go over our homework."

Staring at her oldest daughter Alice replied, "Well, I suggest you join your brother and start doing what I asked you to. The quicker you get this done, the sooner you can call your friend."

Hurston stared at her younger sister with disdain. Toni fought the urge to mock her sister's discomfort. Past situations involving Hurston had convinced her the eldest McDonald sibling knew how to make her life difficult. Returning to their checkers game in her room, Toni watched Octavia's lips form a perfect pout while she considered her next move. The longer she watched her mouth, the more it seemed this funny feeling gathered strength in Toni's stomach. It was just something about Octavia that made her feel strange. Not a bad strange, like when she ate Hurston's first attempt at making a cake. She felt fluttery, like when Hughes pushed her almost too high on the swing in the front yard. Just being near Octavia had her feeling like the day before her birthday. Toni thought about asking her brother what could this mean. After all, Hughes was much nicer and was always reading. He also didn't make her feel like she was stealing his joy when she asked him questions, unlike Hurston. Still, she didn't know if she had words enough to describe it. All she knew, she liked having Octavia near her—even if that meant letting her cheat at checkers.

"Crown me," Octavia said triumphantly.

Looking down at the black-rimmed disc, Toni considered correcting her friend. Octavia obtained her marker's current position through an illegal jump. Still, looking at the smile on her friend's face, it was worth placing one of her captured tokens on top.

"I hereby crown you Queen Octavia, ruler of the checkerboard," Toni announced dramatically.

Giggling, Octavia expressed her thanks and then extended her hand. The two of them had seen the action in a movie they watched in school. A knight had kissed the hand of his queen to show his loyalty. Toni looked down at the smooth nut-brown hand and decided a kiss on the hand wouldn't do.

"Oh," Octavia said following Toni's spontaneous kiss. "Why did you do that?"

"I just felt like it."

"My mommy said girls shouldn't kiss girls. My aunt kisses girls and mommy doesn't let her come visit us anymore. She told me that my aunt does bad things and she doesn't want me to grow up like her."

A cold cloud of fear descended on Toni. 'Did I do something bad?' she thought. 'Is Octavia not going to be my friend anymore? I just wanted to let her know how much I liked her.'

"I'm sorry, Octavia. Please don't tell anyone," Toni stammered. "I promise I will never ever do it again. Cross my heart and hope to die."

Toni could read the struggle in Octavia's face. It probably matched the emotions swirling in her mind about what had just happened. Toni's mother calling them to come take their evening showers before bedtime interrupted the scenario. Since Octavia was a guest, she was to go first, then Toni. Sitting on her bed waiting for her friend to return, Toni felt her stomach sink to the floor. She had done a bad thing. Kissing girls was wrong. Now her friend was going to hate her and never want to come over to her house again. Tonight was supposed to be so much fun and now she had ruined it. Maybe they should have just played the board game Octavia had suggested, then maybe this wouldn't have happened. If only she had a do-over, if only she had one more…

…

"*One more* word from you Toni and you can just kiss Wilmington goodbye."

"But Mom, it's not fair. You let Hurston go to the beach for the weekend when she was my age," the exasperated 16-year-old said to her mother making sure her tone didn't reveal just how frustrated she felt. Standing in her room, she was in the midst of packing when her mom decided to drop a bombshell that her trip might have to be postponed due to some nonsense about her making a D in trigonometry. A slight March breeze tugged gently at the curtains at her open window.

"That's because I went with the Science Club and it was a chaperoned trip. You're just going down to hang with your fast-ass friends," Hurston said. The Bennett College senior had driven down for the weekend and Toni was counting down the hours, minutes, and seconds before she headed back to Greensboro.

"For your information, we are going on a college tour UNC Wilmington is having for minority students," Toni said, looking over her mother's shoulder at her older sister standing in the hallway.

"Mom, it's just going to be overnight and two of the girls from the Blue Revue are driving down with Pearl and me. We are going to do the college tour, take in some of the sites in Wilmington, and be back by Sunday afternoon," Toni said. "You and Daddy agreed to this last month and both of you said how good it was I was starting to take an interest in colleges."

"I have no problem remembering conversations, so you don't have to remind me what I did or didn't say. But that was before I got this progress report. I thought that Pearl girl was supposed be tutoring you in math."

'Yes, she is teaching me some things,' Toni thought, 'but it's not what you going to find in any Wake County high school textbooks.'

"She is tutoring me and my grades are going up. It's just that the first tests I took before she started brought my grades down. Trust me, you will see an improvement by the end of the semester."

"I know that's what you say, but it's just something about the Pearl girl I don't like. I just can't put my finger on it," Alice said, looking at her daughter suspiciously.

Toni fought back a smile; if only her mother knew the truth about Pearl. She was the junior class secretary, first chair violin in the school's orchestra, and Toni's undercover girlfriend. The two connected during tryouts for the school's Drama Club sophomore year. Neither was selected, but found consolation over a shared plate of cheesy fries during lunch the next day. Soon, they began studying after school and hanging out during the weekend. Pearl introduced her to free museum exhibits, budget film matinees at the local independent movie theater on Glenwood Avenue, and the art of people watching at the local flea market. The svelte Asheville native gave Toni her first sexual experience during a rainy Saturday afternoon. Pearl was gentle and patient. Before she did anything, she asked permission. She didn't put her fingers *there* until she was certain Toni was comfortable. Being with Pearl felt like she was walking above the earth. Toni researched the feelings she had for Pearl and knew the proper term. Lesbian. She wasn't a "dyke" or "bull-dagger"— words her mother and her friends tossed out casually about women from their church they didn't like. Pearl empowered her to put a name to the feelings she had in elementary school. Toni couldn't get enough of Pearl. She felt like Celie and Pearl was her Shug. The two planned this overnight visit like WWII Allied strategists. She just *had* to go on this trip.

"The two of you seem to be spending a lot of time together. All this studying after school and going out on the weekends. Something in my spirit tells me there is something more than just going to the movies and some museums between that girl and you."

Toni met her mother's glance hoping she couldn't read her thoughts. The phone rang and broke the spell. Her father's voice rose up the stairs and announced the phone was for her mother.

Toni fought every fiber not to squeal. When Pearl and she were together, it was like everything was brighter and sharper. She inspired her to pay more attention to the world around her and to think about how she wanted to live her life. While she hadn't worked up the courage to have "the conversation" with her parents like Pearl did, Toni knew her time was coming.

Seeing her mother retreat down the stairs, Toni resumed packing with a lighter heart. Sitting down on the bed and fixing her with a knowing look, Hurston interrupted her joy.

"Toni, you may be able to fool Mom, but I know what you are about. For as long as you been able to walk, you have talked about going to NC A&T or another HBCU. You're not interested in UNC Wilmington. This is about you and that girl spending time together."

"It is not."

"It is too. If Mom finds out, it will kill her. You know she stopped speaking to Miss Virginia when she left her husband for that woman ten years ago and that was her best friend. Your mother is all about her Bible and it clearly states homosexuality is a sin before God," she said, putting a sarcastic spin on the last words.

Toni's heart felt heavy. As much as she wanted to dismiss Hurston's words, she knew she spoke the truth.

"Personally, I don't care who you date, but Alice isn't about that life. As long as you live under her roof, I would advise you to chill with whatever you and Pearl have going on," Hurston said, getting up and walking out the room.

Toni sat on her bed and pondered what she should do. Senior year was just three months away and then she would be free. All she had to do was just make it one more...

...

"*One more* word about that gay mess and you can forget about me paying for your college. I didn't sacrifice all those years on the job for you to take my money and make a fool out of me," Toni's mother said to her defiantly standing 21-year-old daughter.

"Mama, being myself is not a bunch of gay mess. It is who I am. You not paying my tuition is not going to change that."

The two McDonald women were standing face to face in a North Carolina A&T University dorm room trying not to break a sweat. Less than thirty minutes prior, Toni had been on top of the world. She was enjoying her summer school experience, her relationship with her royal blue and gold wearing sorority girl was going well, and she had just cashed her first check from her internship. That was until she walked into her dorm room and found her mother standing there with a copy of the school's newspaper in her hand. The top story headline read *NC A&T Opens LGBTQ Center* with a big picture of the center's new intern helping to decorate the office.

"Look at this. Do you know how embarrassing it was to get this in the mail? Good thing your Aunt Janice thought to mail me a copy of this or I may not have known what you are doing up here instead of getting your lessons. I didn't dare tell your father."

ONE MORE

Over her mother's shoulder, Toni could see her roommate acting like she was so into her studies. Any other time, she would have been in Winston-Salem with her boyfriend but, of course, she had to be here to let her mother in and stick around for the fireworks.

Toni couldn't fight the urge to roll her eyes. 'That's it,' she thought, 'Janice is definitely not getting a holiday card this year.' She considered telling her mother that she need not worry about telling her father about her being a lesbian. He already knew. She shared that part of her life last summer. He was a little taken aback, but he accepted it. He told her that his love for her was unconditional. If only her mother had the same attitude.

"Momma, I earned a three point eight GPA last semester, so my sexuality is not impeding on my studies. As you can tell, I have a job so I can put some money aside to help with the fall tuition or get it from somewhere else. I'm sorry you are embarrassed about me being honest about myself, but I can't keep the true me a secret."

"You mean you aren't ashamed being the way you are? You are proud of going against God by cavorting around with women? God speaks about this in Leviticus and Romans. As if you don't have it hard enough being a Black woman in a white man's America, you have to add this one to it."

"No, I'm not ashamed of being who I am, an intelligent woman with a great sense of humor, a belief in doing right by people, and I can make a mean sweet potato pie. I'm a good person and you know that me being a lesbian doesn't change any of that. If someone would have asked you about me the day before you got that article, you would have probably been bragging about how your baby was going to be a big-time engineer. I know you would have because Hurston tells me that's all you do when you run into people at church," Toni said, reaching into her dorm refrigerator to get her mother a bottle of water.

"You leave your sister out this. She is doing what a woman is supposed to be doing. She finished college, got a good job and a steady boyfriend with a good future ahead of him." She refused to take a sip of water even though beads of sweat peaked around her hairline. "I drove up here today to at least give you a chance to apologize for making a mockery of everything I tried to raise you up to be. I should have saved my gas. Be thankful your summer school tuition check has cleared, but if I were you, I would see about getting some more hours at that 'job' you call yourself having. Not a dime of mine is going to be used to promote wicked behavior. Best of luck to you," her mother said grabbing her purse.

Watching her mother walk out, Toni noticed she hadn't taken her bottle of water. Meeting her roommate's eyes, she felt at loss for words. Maybe she could have been a little less brash with her words. If only she had taken the chance to explain to her mother how free she felt. That despite the dirty looks and comments she had received on this historically black campus where three generations of her family had attended, she felt good about being the person she knew herself to be.

"Dang, I can't believe you spoke up to your mom like that. You are a better woman than me," her roommate said. Toni read a sense of newfound respect in her eyes.

"I guess. All I was doing was just standing up for myself. Because if you can't do it for yourself, why should you expect someone else to have your back? I love my mom, but I love myself more. I can't let anyone down me for being me."

Toni's roommate seemed to accept her explanation and returned to her books. While her words may have seemed self-assured, her heart was hurting from her mother's reaction. 'I'm glad Mom finally knows,' she thought, 'but would it have been so bad for her not to know just so I could be her little girl just one more...?

ONE MORE

...

"*One more* day of being single then it's going to be clank, clank," Hughes said, smiling at his younger sister.

"Hey, don't scare her, let her discover the joys of being someone's ball and chain for herself," Hurston said, rubbing her eighth month and counting pregnant stomach. The three were sitting around Toni's Charlotte home, finishing dinner and teasing each other about the end of her impending single status. Thanks to the Supreme Court decision seven months ago, the small ceremony she and Gwyn had originally planned had now grown to a full-fledged legally recognized event set to take place a little over twenty-four hours from this moment. Her partner made her feel complete in a way no one had before. The two of them could have a lively discourse watching a Presidential debate or lose track of time watching YouTube clips of praise dancing gone wrong.

Hurston and Hughes had arrived the day before to help with last-minute details. It meant a lot for them to be there with her. Hurston actually was the one who introduced her to her soon to be wife. She suggested Toni reach out to Gwyn, her Zeta Phi Beta Sorority, Inc. sister to help secure a location for her engineering firm when she moved to Charlotte.

"Lil Sis knows I'm just messing with her. Being with the one you love for the rest of your days is a wonderful thing that I wouldn't trade for anything in the world," Hughes said.

"I have to tell you, the two of you have been great role models about what it means to be married," Toni said, raising her glass in salute to her twin siblings. "Hurston, you worked two jobs to put Baldwin through law school, and Hughes you decided to be a stay-at-home dad so Audre can put in those long hours at the hospital. If I can be half as good at being married, I will be doing more than all right."

"Well, we all learned from the best. Mom and Dad are coming

up on forty years. That's saying a lot in these days and times," Hurston said, glancing at her watch. "Dang, it's seven already. Let me call Baldwin to make sure he got on the road all right with the girls."

Pulling herself up, she left Hughes and Toni at the table. The two sat silent for a moment, then Toni murmured, "I wish Mom was coming, but I guess that would be asking for too much. I mean, we have come a long way since I graduated. We talk on the phone and she did visit a few times after I got the house. I told her about Gwyn and she didn't have anything too overtly negative to say. But after I told her about the engagement, she told me flat out she wasn't interested in attending. Since then I haven't mentioned anything else about it to her. We still talk on the phone, but the subject never came back up. When I sent the invitation to the house, I just put Daddy's name on it so that she wouldn't get her hands on it and throw it in the trash."

"You don't think she is that hateful do you?" Hughes said.

"No, I don't. Alice is many things, but petty is not one of them. I just wish she would change her mind about coming to the wedding. But wishes only come true in fairy tales."

Toni's doorbell interrupted her thought. Tomorrow was the first day of February and the temperature was close to freezing. A wintry mix hit Charlotte hard a few days ago and the roads were still slightly icy at night. She didn't expect anyone to be at her door, at least not without calling first.

"Toni, will you please get your door? I mean your doorbell is cute, but it's not that cute," Hurston said, entering the living room.

Walking slowly to the door, Toni flicked on her porch light and put her eye to the peephole. Shocked at who she saw on the other side, she flung open to door and greeted the cold air and her guest.

"What are you doing here?" she said to the woman with the gray short Afro. "You should have told me you were coming.

I mean, I'm glad you are here. But I'm just surprised. The last time we talked about the wedding you told me you were against it. What happened?"

Removing her coat while walking into the living room Alice responded, "I would be glad to tell you as soon as I get something hot to drink. Hughes, would you mind making me some tea? The train ride down was lovely, but the cab over has left me rattled."

Fulfilling his mother's request, Hughes walked into the kitchen, followed by Hurston. Toni knew while their bodies weren't in the room, they were listening keenly from the next room.

Sitting down on the sofa Alice explained, "Like I told you the last time we talked about this wedding, I had no intention of coming down here. Up until this morning when your father left to come down here, my mind was made up. Then Janice called and told me that my friend Virginia had died. The two of them were sorority sisters so that's how she heard it. Virginia and I were thick as thieves growing up. You know she was my maid of honor when I married your father. Then she told me she was gay and I cut her out of my life. I was always taught that was an abomination and I couldn't see my friend beyond believing that. Cutting her out of my life hurt something awful, but I thought I was doing the best thing. Over the years, I realized I was wrong about that, but I was still too stubborn to reach out. Now, she is gone and I will never get a chance to say I'm sorry to her." Tears twinkled at the corner of her eyes.

Accepting the cup of tea Hughes offered, she took a sip. The peppermint blend seemed to settle her so Alice continued her explanation.

"I realized I would never get a chance to mend fences with Virginia, but I had a chance to try with you. Thankfully, Amtrack had an afternoon train from Raleigh to Charlotte, so I packed a bag and headed down. I called your father and told him I was coming down and made him promise not to tell you. He was supposed to pick me up from the station, but he is out with one of his college buddies who teaches at Johnson C. Smith and they sounded like they had a little bit too much fun for him to try to get on this icy road to pick me up and bring me over here."

Toni felt her eyes moisten. So many times, she had wept about her mother and their strained relationship and wished there was some way to repair it. It was unfortunate it took the death of her mother's childhood friend to spark the move toward her acceptance, still Toni was grateful for the change.

"Now, I'm not saying I'm totally on board with this gay marriage thing, but I always said I would be present for all my children's big days," Alice said, taking Toni's hand in hers. "Getting married is a pretty big step and I know deep down if I wasn't here I would regret it. I'm an old woman and I'm trying to get away from wishing I had did things differently. Now, tell me about the wedding the two of you are planning for tomorrow."

Toni felt her heart soaring. Surrounded by her siblings and her mom, the four of them laughing and teasing each other as they did years ago, Toni flashed back to the fall night when she first acted on her attraction to females. She had come such a long way from that point. Still, there was so much more left for her to experience, including committing herself to loving another woman for the rest of her life. Toni was beyond excited. Just one more day.

Desk Duty
Faith Mosley

I couldn't remember her name, so I closed my eyes tight for just a moment hoping it would float back into my mind, but it didn't. She murmured something unintelligible and then shuddered suddenly. I looked up from between her legs. My tired eyes traveled the length of her body until I could see her head drifting from side to side. She suddenly smiled and pulled me up so that I was perched above her. We kissed softly and then harder and harder. She held me to her, and I caressed breasts that were soft and wonderful. It had been months since I'd slept with a woman, and years since I'd picked up a stranger. I was ready to sleep, but she pushed me down on the bed and began kissing my neck and breasts. She was young and eager. I closed my eyes and put my hands in her fire red hair. I had gone to the supermarket for coffee. Just a late night run, and I came home with a beauty, a lonely soul like myself.

I woke drenched in sweat, rolled to the side of the bed, sat up and looked over at a beautiful, sleeping woman. What the hell was I thinking? The clock read four on the dot. This was the second time in a week I woke soaked. I needed a cool shower, but my legs felt like lead, and my head hurt. I hit the old fan sitting on my nightstand and aimed it directly at my face. I rubbed my fro and was just starting to feel the floor with my bare toes, and really regain consciousness when the banging began. Some asshole was banging on the door of my trailer. Damnit! I was too frustrated to be scared. I stood up and quickly walked to the door so as not to awaken sleeping beauty. This took about three seconds because I lived in an old Airstream that was only twenty-two feet long. I ripped the door open in my underwear. Teegan Yazzie stood before me with a split lip and a right eye in the process of swelling up.

"George, I need your help," she said and pushed past me as if we were roommates. I looked out into the junkyard just to make sure no one had followed Teegan to my hideaway and quickly spotted two lousy, feral cats lounging on the chassis of a rusted out '57 Chevy. I closed the door on a rooster's first crow and turned to look at Teegan. She had helped herself to the one chair in the tiny living room and was looking at me as if I was late for an appointment. She kept running her hands through her mostly dark hair, but like me, she was on the doorstep of fifty; the gray was easing its way into her life the same way it had eased into mine. I was used to it now. I know who I am when I stand in front of the mirror, but whenever I see a young kid sporting a dark fro, I still remember when.

"I thought you were in jail," I said and walked to my mini kitchen. I should know. I processed her paperwork nearly two weeks ago.

"I got out a few nights ago. I went to find my girl, Marcie, but she was gone and so was my stash." I looked at Teegan and popped two Aleve. I held out the bottle and she took two as well. I gave her water and she sat back down. I pulled a frozen sack of peas out of the freezer built into the mini-fridge and tossed it to her, and she gently placed it over her eye.

"What can I help you with?"

"I need you to find out if Marcie's cheating on me and I need my stash back. That's eleven thousand buckaroos I'd saved up, and I just have a gut feeling she took it."

"That's a lot of money. You ever heard of a bank?"

"I don't trust the white man," she said. I looked at Yazzie cradling the peas against her eye. She reminded me a lot of myself, another butch dyke stumbling through the dark. Never see yourself on TV or in the movies or anywhere, only work jobs that allow jeans every day, isolate and rationalize it, drink, take long walks, try to make a go of it in a world that made you feel increasingly irrelevant. I joined the police force a few years back because I really did want to serve my community, and I was tired of cobbling together low-wage jobs. I wouldn't say my co-workers were fun to hang out with, but I do not regret my choice. Cool uniform too.

"How are you gonna pay me?"

"You find my stash, I'll pay you a thousand bucks. You find out where Marcie is and who she's hanging out with, and I'll pay you an additional thousand." We shook hands. I made coffee and asked a lot of questions. Yazzie sucked down two cups of coffee and then tried to make me believe that the DUI that got her stuck in jail for ten days wasn't her fault. She said a dude in a truck ran her off the road. Yes, she'd been drinking, but no, she wasn't a reckless driver and had been run off the road. I didn't care one way or the other about the DUI. We all make mistakes in life. I'd known Teegan Yazzie since high school. She'd moved to the Midwest from New Mexico, so she seemed like a foreigner to us small town kids. We never really hung out, but we knew who the other one was, and we always said hi if we didn't say anything else. She lived just outside of the city in a small, unincorporated township but said she was staying in town at her aunt's house. She said Marcie lived in River City near the campus and gave me her address. Before she left, I asked her one last question.

"Why me, Teegan?"

She looked at me for a minute and then smiled. "Who else is someone like me gonna ask?"

She walked out the door and then stepped into a battered white Ford Taurus wagon and slowly drove out of the junkyard. I didn't ask her who gave her the black eye because I knew that she hung with unreliable people, and when you hang with unreliable people, you tend to get bruised up. Don't get me wrong. I had feelings, but I didn't want to take on more than was required at the time. I had my own problems.

I walked out into the early morning air and savored the not yet burning hot day that lay before me. My desk duty assignment didn't start for two days, so I figured I could help Teegan. Why not? Maybe I could divert attention away from my menopausal body. Desk duty. Well, I shot a man who attempted to strangle his wife and shoot me with a sawed-off shotgun. It was a clean shot, but it still had to be investigated. The husband is in the hospital with a shoulder wound. His wife sits by his side every day. It was the neighbor who called the police. I answered the call alone because the force is severely short-staffed, so no more partners in cars. We ride solo to stretch out our numbers. It's less safe, but until the department can entice sensible people to risk their lives at work, it's what we have to do. The house was off Gibson in a neighborhood I'm very familiar with. It was my first patrol beat, and there were always a lot of fights to break up. I went to the door calmly and radioed my location. When no one answered the door, I kicked it in and found a middle-aged lady on the floor gagging from a strangle hold and a huge sweaty man wrapped around her like a boa constrictor. When I pulled my weapon, he released her and threw his hands up in the air. I told him to sit on the couch. He complied without incident, and then I asked her if she could speak. When I turned my head to communicate with the victim, the man pulled a rifle from behind the couch. My peripheral vision saved my ass, and I unloaded two bullets. The second one knocked him back and he dropped the illegal shotgun. The woman ran to him and kept saying Darryl over and over again. She cursed me while I called an ambulance. I was taken off patrol while my superiors evaluated my actions. Nobody who likes patrolling the streets wants desk duty, but I knew it was temporary, so I didn't cop an attitude about it.

Soft skin. A round, dark mole on her left shoulder blade. A real beauty. Annabelle was her name. That's what she told me when we both reached for the last bag of ground coffee at the late night mini-mart. Annabelle. Pretty name for a pretty woman. She rolled over, opened her eyes and smiled as I stared down at her. A quick kiss was all I got as she sat up and started pulling on underclothes. Neither of us seemed to know what to say. She just smiled and gave me a slow kiss on the lips before heading down the hall.

I climbed into my shower and finally dealt with my dried night sweat. By the time I was cleaned up, my headache was gone and the sun was coming up. Annabelle's little red car was gone. No love note on the table or paper scrap stuck beneath my windshield wiper. Just tire treads in the dirt and a vacant spot that still felt warm. The bed sheets would keep her scent for me. I'd have that at least.

I own a 1975 Datsun B210 that looks like a rusted out, abandoned car, but this baby could move. There was no heat and the radio was busted, but I didn't have to worry about being killed or blinded by faulty airbags. I took off down the drive and watched dust puff up on either side of the car. Of course, all I could think about was Annabelle's skin and the way she kissed as I drove.

Driving by campus felt weird, made me feel a bit like a fugitive. I had recently attempted to return to graduate school and complete the master's in Sociology I had started eight years ago, but after a semester of navigating APA style and ego maniac, quantitative research obsessed professors, I bailed. Instead, I settled for non-completion and started patrolling the streets of River City.

Marcie's apartment was located in the middle of the student ghetto of River City. It was a small brick building just off Silver Avenue. I parked and didn't bother to lock up. I kept the windows down too. There was a certain freedom in having nothing to steal. The building's main door was open. The heat was already permeating everything, and it was only seven in the morning. I stood in the doorway and saw two doors next to each other with nameplates next to them. Teegan said that Marcie's last name was Jones. I didn't see a Jones, so I walked up the narrow wooden staircase to the left. Same setup as downstairs— two doors. The second door said Jones on the nameplate. I knocked. Nothing. I knocked again. Nothing. The door was locked when I tried it. The hall was silent and empty, so I knelt down. I pulled out two steel picks and worked them into her key slot. I gently opened the door. Picking locks was not something I did on a regular basis, but I learned how to do it during a locksmith apprenticeship. Another failed career path.

I walked inside. The windows were up and a gentle breeze blew through the one room apartment. There was a saggy, unmade futon on the floor, a TV on a stand not far from the futon, a bookshelf comprised mostly of lesbian erotica and a collection of adult videos. I noticed two plants on a stand near the window. I felt the soil and it was moist. Marcie had been here recently. The bathroom had a seashell themed shower curtain and a conch shell behind the toilet, a load of cosmetics on the counter, and a magazine on the floor. I was trying to figure out the name of the magazine when the room started spinning. I reached for my phone, but I couldn't seem to locate my pockets. The room swam and I knelt down. *Travel and Leisure: Experience Turkish Delights.* I crawled out to the main room and laid down on the futon. It smelled of sweet perfume. I closed my eyes until the room stopped spinning. I took deep breaths and tried to embrace the vertigo that swept into my life, riding the winds of the climacteric, the change of life. I had always looked forward to the end of menstruating, but the process of getting to the very end was one interesting trip. The room swirled like a whirling dervish when I tried to sit up, so I laid back down. I had no idea how I would explain why I was on this bed if Marcie or anybody else walked in. I closed my eyes and just gave in. The next time I tried to stand, the room slowed down and then finally stopped. I let my eyes sweep over the little apartment one more time before leaving.

At the bottom of the steps I watched a few college girls cruise by on long skateboards laughing. Their long hair blowing in the wind. They wore ripped jean shorts and tank tops. I don't remember ever being that carefree. I guess I never felt the street was put there for me. I just did my best to look "normal." I rolled up my sleeves and climbed into the Datsun and drove to the coffee shop around the corner. I knew the crowd there was unwashed and matlocked, but I wanted a maple syrup scone and another cup of coffee. I had to regain equilibrium.

I sat at a table in the corner and watched skinny White kids in dirty, torn jeans cling to one another and twist each other's hair while standing in line waiting to order. The boys looked as lost as the girls and just as emaciated. Tattoos and earplugs abounded. Weird generation. I punched in Teegan's number, sipped my coffee and waited. An elderly woman's voice came on the phone and said something in a language I didn't know, and then Teegan came on.

"Who was that?"

"That was my aunt," she said.

"What language was that?"

"Dine," she said. "What's up?"

"Marcie's not home, and I want to know exactly why you think she took your wad."

"She knew I had saved a lot, and she was pissed at me."

This was new information that she had failed to tell me back at the trailer.

"Go on," I said.

"Okay. She knew I was sort of having a thing with someone very recently," she said.

"So, before you went to jail?"

Teegan grew silent and I waited patiently. I bit into my maple syrup scone and sipped more coffee. No hurry. The dirty patrons crept in like zombies with cell phones. They hugged each other and talked about whatever happened last night.

"Okay, George. I slept with my alcohol counselor in lock up."

What could I say to that? How many mistakes had I made in my own life? Too many to count. When I left the café I had a new suspect in my head, but I still needed to locate Marcie.

I wanted to earn two grand. I needed the money. I had student loans to repay. The police didn't offer me the loan repayment incentives they now offer new recruits. I was very lucky with housing as my mother is the legal owner of the Black Cat Junkyard. It was left to her in her brother's will. My mother and I had attempted living together as adults after she had a minor heart attack, but her constant critique of my men's underwear along with my choice in women forced my hand, and so I live at the dump. As long as I keep the weeds and vermin at bay, I get to crash in the trailer. That's the deal, and though my mother is a difficult and complex human being, I made sure I kept my end of it. After a day of patrol, I really appreciated the quiet solitude of an abandoned junkyard.

I entered the downtown Metro Detention facility with a mission. My gut told me this counselor woman was involved. She had left her professional judgment at the door when she slept with a prisoner, and Teegan may not have been the only one. This may be her twisted, undiagnosed compulsion. A detention center employee, who at first "sirred" me and then apologized when I said my name was George, instructed me to empty my pockets into a plastic tub, while a uniformed Black man waved a metal wand around my body. I was allowed to pick up my wallet and change. The cell phone and keys stayed with them. An administrative person told me that in the future I needed to make an appointment to see Dr. Gebhard, but since I was a cop and she was there at this very moment she would meet with me. I plopped down into a hard, plastic prison chair and waited. There were no magazines to peruse, just concrete block walls painted eggshell. Standard institutional décor to make sure you feel really bad about yourself.

A door opened and a pair of Dansko clogs moved in my direction. The shiny brown clogs were worn by a blonde woman with piercing blue eyes. She had a professional smile that masked a raging libido. She immediately reminded me of my ex, Ramona, who operated a non-profit in bifocals and sensible clothes, but when she got home, look out. I stood up and smiled back. I extended my hand and felt hers clasp mine. Her hand was moist and limp. I was definitely suspicious. I followed her into the office that was also painted eggshell but decorated with landscape paintings to evoke a sense of calm, I guessed, and real seashells perched on top of the bookshelves and file cabinets. Dr. Gebhard smiled again, but this time the smile was tighter. I was evaluating her, and I think she felt it.

"So, Officer Black, is it? What can I do for you?" It was hard to speak to this woman who was wearing the sexiest footwear in the world and who had recently been lying sweaty and naked in bed or on this very floor with Teegan Yazzie. I reminded myself that I had been hired, albeit with no retainer, but I was on the clock so to speak.

"I'm investigating a case, and I thought you might be able to help me." This was obviously not official police business, but she didn't need to know that.

"I don't know how I can help." She wasn't smiling now. Her

forehead lines creased, and she suddenly looked ten years older than she did in the hallway. She paced while I got comfortable in a leather winged back chair, and then the kindly assistant brought in a tray with coffee. It was going to take more than a moment for me to convince this strange woman that she could trust me.

"Teegan Yazzie, does that name sound familiar? She told me you were her counselor while she was here. She said you helped her come to terms with some issues that may have contributed to her drinking problem." Dr. Gebhard nodded as I spoke. She seemed relieved by what I was telling her. I wasn't accusing her of anything. I was getting her to relax. I let the words sink in, and then I looked around the room. I noticed a *Let's Go Istanbul Guide* on her desk and the expensive-looking turquoise labyris pendant dangling from a leather cord around her neck. I also noticed faint perspiration collecting in the exact spot where she would receive a tracheotomy if ever she needed one. Dr. Gebhard was nervous. I work patrol. I'm not even a detective yet. That's my goal, but I've watched enough people being questioned. I've studied how the good investigators work a case.

"I really cannot divulge much information. I only saw Teegan six times. It's unethical for me to assist you any further regarding a specific client." Her eyes moved to the door, but I stayed seated and poured myself more coffee. Perspiration formed on her upper lip. I thought about the clogs, and then I got reckless.

"I think we both know ethical behavior took a hike a long time ago." She looked less mean now. Oddly, she smiled a closed mouth smile and stood up. Now I felt scared. She walked over to where I was sitting and dug her long, sensual fingers into my fro. She started messing up my hair, and then I felt a soft downy cheek against my neck. She tried to kiss me, but I jumped up out of the seat. Seduction was a game to her, and I didn't want to play.

The room was windowless. She pushed me against a row of filing cabinets. A shell fell to the concrete floor and shattered into fragments. She had her hands on my shoulders and wasn't smiling at all. In fact, she looked evil. I was stuck against the ropes as we say in the boxing world. She had me. I looked down for a brief moment and caught the glow of newly burnished brown clog leather standing amongst the shattered shell bits. When I looked back into her eyes, everything was a blur. Her mouth was on mine and she was panting like a wild dog. I kissed her back and I felt her tongue plunging into my mouth. Like a drunken miner, it was up against my gums and interior cheek walls. I was as disgusted with myself as I was turned on.

We fell to the floor and I tried to slow this ridiculous situation down, but in that very moment, I was overcome with a bout of menopausal-induced vertigo and I couldn't stand. The room began to spin and I was overcome with nausea. Dr. Gebhard ripped off her blouse, sending fake pearl buttons flying into the air. She unsnapped her front-hinged beige lace bra and attempted to force an erect pink nipple into my mouth when my stomach locked. The room spun on faster and faster, and I was on my knees when the fire hose gush of vomit flew from my mouth all over her beautiful blonde head and body. She screamed wildly, the room continued to spin for me, and I threw my arms out in front of me for balance. The door opened and the administrative assistant ran in and screamed when she saw her kindly doctor half naked and covered in vomit. I grabbed a chair to steady myself. The nausea subsided as quickly as it came. Dr. Gebhard rushed from the room with the stunned assistant in tow, and I turned and leaned on the cabinets. In the ensuing confusion, caused mostly by the assistant's manic screams, I was rushed out of the building and found myself standing on the concrete bridge clutching the railing in an attempt to steady my legs. When I finally sat down in my little car, I exhaled. It was good that I'd taken this case. I needed the money, the action, and a wake-up call. I am not in control of the shifting tides within my body, an orchestral symphony that has grown more complex and that I no longer conduct—if I ever did. Menopause is a trip.

Gebhard was easy to follow. I'd pulled into the street just outside of the secured staff-only lot and waited. I knew she'd need a shower after that nightmare. She entered a late model Volvo and drove cautiously east on Lomas and then turned on Pennsylvania. She pulled into the driveway of a neat Arts and Crafts bungalow that was lovingly landscaped with rose bushes lining the drive. I drove past her house and parked around the corner. I sat there for about three minutes spitting out the vomit aftertaste clinging to my mouth and then stepped out into the heat of the day. I casually walked through a side gate that led to the backyard of her house. I could hear shower water running as I passed the bathroom window. I looked around the yard and decided the big hedge that was almost flush with the high-back wall would be perfect. I squeezed between the hedge and the wall and waited. She showered and left the house in under twenty minutes. I entered through the backdoor with an elbow to the glass. I walked inside and went straight to the bedroom. She had a bag packed and her *Let's Go Istanbul* was on the dresser next to a passport and a bulging black leather sack. I didn't even need to open it to know the remaining money was inside. Gebhard was a compulsive sex addict who obviously didn't discriminate between butch and femme.

I go with my gut now that I'm older and wiser. I used to hear it, but wisdom is often wasted on the young and headstrong. The sexy Danskos were the tipoff. Those were expensive shoes, and I knew a counselor could certainly afford to purchase new shoes on a good salary, but it was the timing and the store fresh newness of them. Marcie's *Travel and Leisure: Destination Turkey*. People always broadcast their moves. That's what Alvino, my old boxing coach used to tell me. He'd say, "Just watch and wait. In the end, everybody wants to tell you what they're gonna do." I punched in the number for Teegan. I knew I didn't have much time. Dr. Gebhard wasn't gonna take too long to run her errands.

Teegan arrived at Gebhard's bungalow just after Marcie. She stepped out of the Taurus looking confused about why she was here until she saw Marcie's pink scooter. I met her at the door to defuse the potential explosion.

"What the hell's going on, George?"

"You owe me two thousand bucks," I said. Marcie stepped out from behind me. Her mascara had run down her face during the tear-filled excuses about psychological seduction and never being loved right.

Now she just looked like a neglected child who got carried away in her mother's makeup kit.

"Forgive me, Teegs. You're the only one who understands me." Teegan threw her arms around the trembling Marcie. People are so predictable.

When Dr. Gebhard stepped into her living room ten minutes later, she stood absolutely still as she dropped a Walgreens bag full of travel-size shampoo and conditioner bottles and watched her former client/lover embracing her current, sad-clown-faced lover. The whole scene was disturbing and I wanted to go home. Teegan walked me back to the Datsun and paid me two thousand dollars cash from the black bag. She shook my hand solemnly. I didn't even ask her what she was going to do about Dr. Gebhard or Marcie.

I drove away feeling a little sad about the whole affair. On the drive back to my place, I passed my ex's apartment and was tempted to stop in and finish what got started with the good doctor. Instead, I followed my gut and drove on.

Maggie Chu is my best friend. Like me, she was a non-completing, academic failure and slow to accept the fact that she did not have forever to find a suitable career. Maybe because of these facts, she was my only friend in life. She worked at her uncle's restaurant where she waited tables in jeans, a white shirt and black tie. It was a slow night, so she agreed to meet me at The Wise Owl, a lesbian bar since 1961. No matter what storm raged out in the world, the safety of its warm, dark, woman-loving interior was a constant. Maggie sat next to me at the bar, and we sucked down a new local microbrew. I told her about the case and how I kissed a crazed mental health professional and then threw up all over her. As expected, she was nonplussed. Maggie has weathered life's potholes and keeps on rolling. Her short, dark hair was now an even salt and pepper, and she had shed most illusions about life. I was tired and glad to be looking at a sane face.

"So Ramona was asking about you—" Maggie paused and waited for my reaction. I nodded. "She said something about disappearing cats and how she may want to hire you."

"Another case already." We raised our glasses in sleepy agreement.

With this new investigation sideline, desk duty may not be such a bad thing after all. I closed my eyes for a moment and imagined having Annabelle again and again. Chet Baker wafted from the jukebox, *Imagination is funny. It makes a cloudy day sunny.*

Epiphany

S. Andrea Allen

I knew it was time to leave when she put her hands around my neck.

Jordan is a compulsive gambler, a fact she kept from me until I had moved across the country to be with her. I'd actually never been in a casino before I met her, so I thought going for my birthday would be fun. It was, and it was fun the next time we went, and even the next. I won $500 the first time I ever played a slot machine, and I didn't see the harm in going every now and then. Over time, though, our date nights became casino nights, and our $50 budget became "How much money do you have left in your account?" and "I'll pay you back when I get paid." We gambled all night, sometimes stopping for a meal at the buffet, sometimes not. When I got tired of the flashing lights and the incessant dings of the slot machines, I'd go read a book in the deli. More often than not, Jordan would find me and beg for my ATM card. More often than not, I'd give it to her.

It wasn't always like this. In fact, our relationship was quite normal, at first. We were both degreed professionals: Jordan was a professor of anthropology at a research university in the Pacific

Northwest, and I was a former teacher, trying to figure out what to do with my life after leaving a job I hated. I was in a state of flux, and Jordan's offer to come live with her seemed like the answer to my problems.

I loved teaching, but hated public schools, and the master's degree in History I had left corporate America for was only good for a couple of things: teaching or as a springboard into a doctoral program. I had vowed to never teach in public schools again unless I was starving or couldn't pay my rent, and at the rate we were going, it seemed I'd have to dust off my resumé and hit up the local teaching job fair soon. At the moment, I was taking classes at the university where Jordan worked, as well as working part-time at a local non-profit. But that didn't pay much, and I knew I couldn't rely on Jordan to pay my bills.

I had only been out here with Jordan for four months when things started to go horribly wrong. We were on one of our Friday night "dates" and I had just won about $800 on a slot machine. I quickly cashed out my ticket and put the money in my purse. I was done gambling for the night. Before I could find a spot to sit down in the deli, Jordan walked up.

"Did I just see you at the cashier? How much did you win?" I could see her eyes glazing over at the thought of more money to feed into the slot machines, chasing the elusive "big hit."

"Not that much," I replied warily. I was trying to figure out how she'd spotted me and if she'd seen the cashier count out my winnings. I didn't want to lie, but I didn't want her to know how much money I'd won either. I was saving up to move, but Jordan didn't know that yet. Plus, I was tired of feeding her gambling habit. It was like she had a sixth sense for sniffing out my money. I'd already blown my savings and my fuck you money (my emergency travel and relocation fund), and I was determined to keep this little bit of cash to myself.

"Well, give me a hundred dollars. I'm broke, Trish."

"What makes you think I have that much?"

" 'Cause I know *you*, Trish, now give me some money!"

We were standing in the aisle, between the cashier's booth and a row of machines, and I saw a few people glance our way. I didn't want to make a scene, so I handed her a crisp one-hundred dollar bill, making sure to keep the rest of my cash out of sight. I hoped she'd win something so we could go home. Or lose it all; I didn't care. I just wanted to get out of here.

"I only won two hundred, so if you lose that, I don't have anything else to give you," I lied.

She smiled and hurried off, ready to get back to the action. I stood there shaking my head, trying to figure out how I'd gotten myself into this mess.

...

I met Jordan at a party several years ago, and we connected over drinks and crappy hors d'oeuvres. She was cute; light brown skin, short sandy hair, and an infectious smile and laugh. She was a little short for my taste, (I liked my women tall), but under the covers, it's all the same, so it was all good. I was kind of turned on by the fact that she had a Ph.D. and was an assistant professor at some far-away college in the Pacific Northwest. I was thinking about graduate school myself, and we were able to talk in depth about the struggles Black women faced in the academy. Over time, our relationship blossomed, and although we encountered a few rough spots, I thought we could work it out. Now that I think about it, we had some *really* rough spots, like the time she came to visit and within four hours I was tossing her luggage out of my room and screaming at her to get out. See, Jordan was an asshole. Cute and smart for sure, but an arrogant asshole. She could also be mean, although at the time, I had no idea how mean she could be.

EPIPHANY

There were other red flags: Jordan told me she had "attach-
ment" and "abandonment" issues, which I now realize was just
code for "I am incapable of sustaining a committed relationship,"
but I didn't know that at the time. Then, I thought I could love
her through it, because clearly I was suffering from Florence
Nightingale Syndrome. A match made in heaven, right? She
told me that she had been in therapy and was making "excellent
progress" (she wouldn't lie about that, would she?), so I figured
it was okay. Jordan was also a smoker. Virginia Slims were her
brand, and out of respect for me, she never smoked inside, even
in her own house. Although I hated the smell and residual taste of
cigarette smoke, you know, that smoky taste of menthol, carbon
monoxide, and nicotine, I thought smokers were sexy. I suppose
I saw one too many Kool cigarette ads in *Ebony* magazine when
I was a kid.

Over the course of several months our relationship blossomed
and I made my way out to visit Jordan. I met her colleagues and
she showed me around her mid-sized town. I absolutely loved
this part of the country, and her house was in a cute little valley
with gorgeous mountain views. I was beginning to entertain the
idea of moving in with her and the region was a plus. One of the
places we visited while I was there was the casino. There were a
couple of Indian casinos in the area, and we went to one closest
to town. At some point we traveled to casinos all over the region,
but this was my first visit ever to an actual casino. I was raised
in a pretty conservative Christian household and gambling was a
no-no. Never mind the fact that I was lesbian, gambling was just
something that I could never admit to experiencing to my family.
But more than that, I just couldn't see giving my money away.

Eventually, Jordan convinced me to move in with her. I was
hesitant to move so far away from my family and friends, and
I'd also be leaving a good-paying job as a counselor at a public
school. As much as I hated that job, it kept me close to the people

I loved. My gut told me to stay put, but my brain had decided that it was time for a change and that this was the change I had been looking for. I also loved her, a little. So I packed up my house, put my things in storage, and flew across the country to be with the woman I intended to spend the rest of my life with.

...

"Fat bitch! What you crying for, bitch?" Jordan screamed at me as I sat crying silently on the sofa.

The past two months had been hell. After fighting about money and her gambling for weeks, we had decided to call it quits. The relationship just wasn't working out. The problem was that I lived in her house. With my help, she had gambled away my savings and I didn't make enough money to live on my own in this area. I had given her money, loaned her money, and each time, she had promised to give it back. Now, most of my fuck you money was gone, and the relationship was busted. I was trapped and she knew it. Most of the time she was away for work, this or that conference, this or that meeting, and I'm guessing she used pay advances to cover her expenses for travel— because I knew her money was tight. It was hard to believe that she made over six figures a year but had to borrow money from me to help cover the basics. It was peaceful while she was away, and I had been planning my escape. I had applied to and been admitted to a graduate program back East, and she was mad about it. She was also pissed because I had called her out of an important meeting to tell her that the lights at the house had been turned off due to non-payment. The problem was, I had been giving her money for the power bill for six months and I always paid her on time. I had never seen a bill though, so I had no idea that she hadn't been paying the bill. That was, of course, until I came home and found the red disconnect notice on the door.

EPIPHANY

I wasn't crying because I was sad or upset. I was just so angry I didn't know what to do, so I did nothing. My silence enraged her; I could see her chest heaving and hear her breathing go ragged. Suddenly, Jordan reached over, grabbed my neck, and started choking me. I struck out at her with my fists, but the blows seemed to bounce right off of her. She shifted to try to tighten her grip, and somehow I was able to knee her in the groin. She gasped and let go just long enough for me to punch her in the face. I jumped up, and gasping for air, I ran to my room and slammed the door. I was in shock; I couldn't believe this woman had put her hands on me. If I wanted to be truly honest with myself, I had to admit that Jordan had tried to kill me. Things were bad for sure, but I never thought it would come to this.

As the shock of what had just happened started to wane, I started to try and formulate a plan. I had always been the kind of person who could remain calm in a crisis, although I was usually solving other people's problems, not my own. I got on the computer and started typing. I needed to find a place to stay, and I needed to find one right now. I had begun a new fuck you money account and I could probably find a small studio apartment. The only problem was that I had just found out that I had been accepted into graduate school, and I really couldn't afford to move twice. Still, I had to try. I couldn't stay here. I had just picked up my cell phone to call about an apartment when Jordan appeared in the doorway.

"So what are you doing, calling the police? I'll just tell them you hit me too." Jordan stood in the doorway looking over at me. Her bravado was false; I could see the fear in her eyes and I knew she was really afraid that I'd call the police. She had much more to lose than I did, including her beloved tenure-track job at the university, and she knew we'd both be arrested if I called the police. But I didn't give a damn about her job, or what would happen if she got arrested for assaulting me. I just wanted to get away from her for good.

My purse and keys were on the kitchen counter, so I grabbed them and left the house without a word. Jordan was on the patio smoking a cigarette. I had no idea where I was going, but I knew I needed to process what had just happened and try to figure out what to do. I had tried to make it work with her, and had even gotten her to go to Gambler's Anonymous meetings. I went, too, because I was co-dependent and an enabler. I needed help just as much as she did. But I also knew that I didn't love her enough to stay in this relationship, and I needed to save myself.

I drove around for a while and eventually stopped at the park to try to come up with a plan. I loved this place, although now I cannot recall its name. There was a beautiful trail that backed up to a little pond. The park sat in a little valley surrounded by rocky hills, and there was even a little waterfall that fed the pond. Sometimes, I'd just sit and watch the turtles, and sometimes, when I was feeling frisky, I'd try to jog a little. It was so peaceful here, and it was hard to imagine that my girlfriend had nearly choked me to death just a couple of miles away.

I couldn't tell anyone what had happened. None of my friends had wanted me to leave, and I really didn't want to tell them that they had been right. I knew that was my pride talking, but I still couldn't do it. I was a highly educated Black woman and I should have known better. I had mentioned to my friend Jay that we had been having trouble a few weeks back, and he just kept encouraging me to try to make it work.

"No one asks you to move that far away just to give up," he'd said. What I couldn't tell him was that neither one of us wanted to make it work. We *couldn't* make it work. There was nothing to save.

It was starting to get dark, and I began making my way back toward the house. I looked around at the beautiful firs and the lush mountain valley; late spring was absolutely gorgeous here. I knew it was likely that I'd never see this part of the country again if I left, but I was okay with that. I'd known for a while that I would leave Jordan, but I never thought it would be because she assaulted me. Our relationship was long dead, but I thought we could co-habit for a little while until I saved enough money to leave. Her gambling was still out of control and I couldn't save her. I could only save myself. I didn't hate her, but I didn't love her anymore either. I partly blamed myself for allowing this mess to drag on for nine months, but I also knew that Jordan had lied to me about the extent of her gambling. I hoped she would get real help, and I knew that I'd never set foot in a casino again. I needed more control over my life than gambling afforded, and I never, ever wanted to be in this situation again.

I pulled into the garage and sat there for a minute. To hell with pride, I wanted to go home. In the morning I would call my best friend and tell her what happened. I knew she'd help me find a place to live until school started. I took a deep breath and got out of the car. It was time.

Two Moons
K.A. Smith

The moon was the only thing that soothed Selene as a child. She was rambunctious, often crying and raging for what seemed like no reason, but immediately silent once under the glow of the moon.

It was the only thing that made her quiet. Looking up at the moon, whether a sliver or the full round. Selene just had to have the moon shining down on her to rest. The thing calmed her so much I wished I could bring it inside the house." Her mother, Judith, would tell the story to anyone willing to listen, describing in detail how taking Selene's white bassinet out to the front yard was the only way she got a much needed rest from the fussy girl. The moment the moon touched little Selene she calmed and relaxed, drifting right to sleep.

When she was old enough, around fourteen, Selene took to sleeping outside in the gazebo every night. She'd drag her mother's old blue and gray sleeping bag out across the lawn, bunch it up in the corner of the structure and nestle in, craning her neck up at the sky.

Her mother didn't much mind. She was sure Selene would grow out of her "moon phase" after a time, much like Bobbi

Donovan two houses down grew out of his obsessive love of dinosaurs and Genevieve from across the street grew out of her "pretty princess phase."

But Selene didn't grow out of it. Rather, she grew *into* it, feeling the heavy pull of the satellite more and more as she matured. The moon had a deep draw on her, more than other people who claimed to be affected by its ever-changing form.

Her desire to be near it, touch it, even kiss it made Selene crazy sometimes, irrational. She would look up, whispering to the moon, "I love you, I love you, I love you" with unexplainable tears in her eyes. When she stood in its light, warmth overtook her body and traveled so deep she felt excited and overwhelmed and everything all at once. There were no words or sounds she could make to explain what she felt, but Selene knew she was supposed to be up in the sky with her beloved moon.

...

It was quite possible the girl was special. The thought crossed her mother's mind from time to time. *Special.* It wasn't right that a child's obsession continued into adulthood. "Shouldn't she have grown out of this by now? Did I do this?" Judith asked herself, thinking of how she used to drag the bassinet out under the sky and allowed the girl to sleep in the gazebo night after night. Had she inadvertently exposed Selene to some sort of harmful moon rays that warped her? Was that even a thing? Judith didn't know, but she worried about her daughter. She was growing into such a beautiful woman, but this obsession made her a standout.

When Judith found Selene naked on the lawn the evening of her eighteenth birthday, she lost all hope that her daughter would ever be normal.

Selene stood in full view of the neighbors beneath the shimmering light humming *Blue Moon* to herself, her hands rubbing her oil-black skin while she sang and smiled at no one in particular and swayed left to right like a night lily in the breeze, wholly encompassed by her task.

"Selene, what are you doing?" Judith looked her daughter up and down, expecting to see some physical damage to explain her behavior. "Come inside, child. Put some clothes on this instant."

"Mother, I have to bathe in the moonlight," she babbled calmly. "I have to spread the moonlight over my skin. I want to smell like the moon. I want to be the moon. I am the moon. Can't you see? This is *love*." Selene continued to smooth her skin, massaging the moonlight like shea butter over her throat, pure bliss spreading across her face.

Judith knew there was no stopping Selene and no telling her that she was, in fact, *not* the moon.

Selene continued on, her behavior driven by a love of the moon and a desire to soak up as much moonlight as possible. Her mother did not pretend to understand, nor did anyone else in her life. She was, to them, strange, on her own planet, in a fantasy world where the moon simply loved her back.

But it was not a fantasy. The moon *did* love Selene.

Luna cherished her more than the night sky itself. From the moment Luna rested her gaze on Selene as a child, she felt a protectiveness that had been reserved only for the stars. As the girl grew into a woman, her upward glances and whispered declarations of love made Luna desperate to know her, to be with her. Luna looked down on her human every night, plotting ways for them to be together and wondering if Selene truly meant it when she looked up at the night sky and said, "I love you." Could she even know how much those sweet words and those wide brown eyes full of admiration focused up meant to a majestic moon? No one had ever shown such love and awe for Luna the way Selene had.

Luna watched for Selene all hours of the night and day, so much that she was often late or did not show at all in other parts of the world, leaving the night skies bleak and black. People began to think the world was ending, but for Luna the world was just beginning. Beginning to have meaning.

"Luna, you look all funny. What gives?"

Luna shot a glance over at Esme, her good friend, a star a few orbits away, then turned her gaze back to Selene. She had fallen asleep in her family's gazebo, like she used to do when she was a child. "Oh, it's nothing."

Esme spun around several times whipping purple gases around like a cape. She was a young star still marveled in her ability to fume. "I think it's that girl down on Earth. What's her name, Star or something?"

"Her name is Selene. She's gorgeous isn't she?" Luna's eyes glazed over with love. If only there was a way for her to swoop down lower for a closer look. But that was almost impossible. Any closer and she would surely disturb the tides.

"Yeah, she's pretty, Luna. But she's human. And she's waaaay down there. And we are waaaay up here."

"I know, I know." Luna sighed. "But I just can't get enough of her. She's so, so…"

"Tiny?" Esme spun around until she was dizzy and let out a high-pitched laugh.

Luna chuckled at Esme's antics. She was supposed to be studying for her galaxy exam and Luna was supposed to be helping her. But Esme seemed more interested in spinning, and Luna was certainly more interested in watching Selene. If only she could absorb the dark-skinned woman's magnificence.

"I think I have a plan, Esme." Luna whispered so lowly, her friend almost didn't hear.

"What do you mean? What kind of plan?" Esme skulked closer, her purple trail of gases fizzling out.

"I'm going to get her up here or me down there. I haven't quite figured it all out yet, but—"

"What?" Esme shrieked. "How do you plan to do that? If you get any closer you'll cause a tsunami or something, wreck the entire coast. You can't, Luna. You *can't*."

Luna heard what Esme was saying, but it didn't matter. She needed to be closer. She had to let Selene know that she heard her words, that she saw her dance, that *she* existed because of her. Luna changed the subject and pointed down around the gazebo. "Look at the moonflowers Selene planted a few days ago. They're my favorite. She knows my favorite flower, Esme. She loves me."

Luna eased her light over the paper-white flowers, touching them gently. Luna felt Esme's tight eyes on her, likely questioning her sanity. She ignored the glare.

"Luna." Esme was persistent. "You're, what? A few billion years old? Do you really think she... I mean she's probably just infatuated, you know. A pagan or something."

Some friend, Luna thought, hitting Esme with a low blast of light to scramble her sense of direction. What did a silly star know? Esme slept all day and spent most of her time fuming out until she was in a daze, winking at airplanes she mistook for other stars.

Luna looked back down at the gazebo, but Selene was not inside. She was awake, standing in front of the structure with a handful of moonflowers. She reached them up toward the sky and smiled. Luna took a deep breath. Never had she felt anything so pure, so powerful and consuming as Selene's affection. Despite Esme, Luna knew. *This is love.*

Luna sighed, looking down. "Selene."

Selene was perfectly placed against the night, a glowing reflection of the moon, her gauzy, white gown flowing around her. She spun around, then kissed one of the flowers she held and offered it up to Luna.

"Oh, Selene. If we could just be together, the world would make much more sense."

Luna inched lower, reaching out to take the flower from

Selene, but they were still much too far apart.

"Luna, don't," Esme warned.

"Shh…" Luna eased forward again.

"Luna, you're getting too close."

"It's fine, Esme. I know what I'm doing."

Luna had no idea what she was doing.

She wasn't sure if she'd explode or disintegrate or what, because anything could happen that close to Earth. The changes in the atmosphere, the tug of energy came on quickly.

But Luna couldn't stop herself. She kept moving, knowing she would soon be able to touch Selene, accept the flower she offered. *Just a little closer…*

Soon she was glowing and radiating light like she'd never felt before. A beam of platinum energy shot out in front of her, creating a path straight down on the ground where Selene stood.

The faint sound of Esme calling her tickled Luna's senses, but she didn't look back. She didn't want to see how far she'd strayed.

"I knew you'd come for me one day." Selene followed the path in front of her and stepped right up to Luna. "People think I'm crazy. But here you are, my love."

"Here I am." Luna didn't know what else to say. She was close enough to feel Selene's breath on her surface. She felt her core heating and cooling rapidly, expanding and shrinking until she felt out of breath and woozy. Her outer edge tingled with a painful pressure, but she couldn't force herself to pull away from Selene.

"Here." Selene reached out placing the moonflower on Luna's head.

The soft petals tickled Luna's surface. It was the most unexpected and exquisite sensation Luna had ever experienced, like what a shooting star must feel when bursting through clouds across the sky. Luna wanted more. She wanted to feel like that all the time. She smiled at Selene and blurted out the first thing that came to mind.

"Come back with me. Come live in the sky with me." She watched Selene's eyes grow wide as she contemplated the words. "You'll be the goddess of my sky."

"And you'll be mine," Selene said softly. She closed her eyes and nodded.

"You mean it?"

"Yes! I am the moon."

"We'll be two moons together."

Luna grinned and widened the path of platinum light, lifting Selene into her magnetic field. They rose from the ground and drifted slowly back into the sky, the wind billowing Selene's dress behind her, like a banner. As they rose higher and higher, Luna memorized every dip and curve in Selene's face, realizing her smile was identical to a crater on her own dark side.

"I've always wanted to fly."

"You're definitely meant for the sky." Luna pulled Selene closer and twirled her around.

"More, more," she giggled, kicking her legs out against the air.

Luna did as she was asked, spinning and twirling Selene across the sky, watching as her smooth skin shimmered and sparkled with stardust.

"Kiss me, Luna. Don't let this be a dream."

A flutter of hesitation swirled inside Luna. She'd never kissed a human before. But, oh, how she wanted to now!

As Luna moved in closer, she caught a glimpse of Esme over Selene's shoulder, twinkling at her highest wattage. She gave Luna the thumbs up, then dimmed her light until she disappeared into the backdrop.

"A kiss under the moon means eternity, Selene. Is that what you want?"

Selene blinked her eyes and nodded. "Kiss me."

TWO MOONS

...

The bright light poured into Judith's bedroom window, waking her suddenly as it blanketed the room in a wide pattern. She rubbed her eyes and sighed with exasperation. *It's probably just someone using our driveway to turn around again.*

A quick flick of the mini blinds and the room would be dark again. Judith got out of bed, peeking through the mini-blinds' slats out of habit. It wasn't a passerby turning around. It was the moon, beaming so loudly that Judith had to squint to continue looking at it. She knew she'd never seen the moon so large and white and... happy?

It seemed unnatural, a little scary even, and yet she was hypnotized. For the first time, she understood her daughter's love for the thing. It was truly majestic. "It's at least twice as big tonight," Judith mumbled, squinting against the light. She craned her neck closer to the window as her eyes adjusted. *Selene?*

"Oh, my God!" Judith burst out onto the lawn in the direction of the gazebo, hoping her tired old eyes were playing tricks on her. But she already knew that was Selene up in the sky, nestled close to the moon. She found the rumpled sleeping bag in the corner of the gazebo, and snapped her attention toward the sky again.

"Oh, Selene."

Judith tried to calm her breath as she watched on, but her heart thumped in her chest. She couldn't believe what she was seeing, and yet she knew it was perfect. The moon spun her daughter around on tiptoe until she was giggling and laughing, the sound ringing of pure joy.

A smile crept across Judith's face as the moon inched closer and closer to Selene. Their kiss shook the atmosphere around her, setting off a brilliant storm of shooting stars.

Her heart filled with love and sadness as she drifted back to the gazebo and sat down, finally calm. She needn't worry about her daughter being normal anymore. She was, indeed, special. Too special to be normal.

Judith blew a kiss up to her daughter. "Goodnight," she whispered and watched the sky transform and stretch to accommodate two moons.

Goldilocs

Jai Allis

When my sister came out to me, I was honored. Honored because she trusted me. We sat barefoot on her porch swing, swaying with the fall breeze, searching between clouds for the cluster of stars we wished upon when we were little. We could have celebrated my week home by hitting the club for a flood of free drinks. No place, however, would have been better than our backyard solitude.

"I knew you'd be okay with it," Tina said.

I turned to her with admiration as she looked at the sky with relief. But why would she doubt my support? Tina meant the world to me. She was successful beyond standard definition. She completed a master's in Educational Psychology by twenty-two. She had landed the best salary and position among her grad school cohort. Soon after graduation, a new car and house followed. She gained distinction (and extra income) by way of speaking engagements. My sister was sincere, dependable, loving, and hard working. And through hard work, she added a doctoral degree to her curriculum vitae three weeks prior to her twenty-eighth birthday.

I looked up to my sister. Despite being three years my senior, we never clung to "big" or "little." We were the dynamic duo and nothing stood between us or our joint plans. As soon as I finished grad school and garnered a little more real-world experience under my belt, I planned to move home and launch a business with Tina to provide direct psych services and customized educational tools.

In the meantime, Tina had to profess her sexuality to me. "This is my bridge to personal completion. Happiness," she explained.

Well…

I didn't know it, but my sister had dated two women before coming out to me. And it wasn't like other folks didn't know already. *We* didn't know. Her family. Where was the honor in that?

I planted my feet to stop the swing. "Oh," I said, disappointed.

I knew Tina felt guilty because she got chatty. She spent twenty minutes telling me about girlfriend number one (the cheater), who "met" another woman on Instagram, and forty-five minutes on number two (the moocher), who lived in her house for a year.

"A whole damn year?" I shouted.

From that night forward, Tina kept me in the loop. Whether she needed an ear to vent or a word of advice, I was only a phone call or text message away. I had my status back. No more secrets between us. The dynamic duo was whole again.

Two years later, I survived and wrapped up grad school. But I was sick of my job. I'd lost track of how many evenings I rushed home to stretch across my bed, complaining to Tina about my culturally incompetent, lazy ass supervisor.

"Leave," Tina said. "Life is too short. I'm ready for you to move back anyway."

The next morning, I quit.

My 1,000-mile journey back home was expensive but worth every penny. I didn't realize how much I missed the familiar sights and surroundings, how much I wanted to trade daily train commutes for strolls to the beach. I also missed the people, the annual cookouts and "how ya doing" I encountered every ten feet. Once home and wrapped in the comfort of slower living, I wanted to hang out with Tina. So, I reached into my wallet and passed her a pair of tickets.

"How in the world did you these?" she asked. "I heard this concert sold out weeks ago."

"I know people who know people."

The interest in Tina's face faded as she handed the tickets back to me. "I can't go. Jade's sick."

Well…

Little did I know, but my sister was eight months into a relationship with girlfriend number three.

"Oh," I said, surprised.

I knew Tina felt bad about the timing of the update because she began to speak in her own defense. "Whenever I talk to you," she said, "we focus on other things. It's not like I wasn't going to tell you about Jade. I just hadn't gotten around to it."

"Around to it?" I rolled my eyes. "The concert is tomorrow. Not today. I'm sure you can spare a few hours."

"No, I can't. She's in my bed and I told her I won't leave her alone this weekend."

I grabbed my purse from the coffee table and marched to the door, offended by the hint of irritation in her voice. When I pulled out the driveway, Tina called to apologize. "I'll make it up to you. Hey! How about I throw you a welcome back party?"

Unfortunately, I had paid $649 for my cell phone. Otherwise, I would've thrown it out the window. Instead, I ended the call without warning. I reacted rudely, but that didn't stop Tina from planning a party for me.

True to her word, Tina gathered about two-dozen family members and friends at her house the following weekend. I hadn't been in the company of so many people I grew up with in years. I didn't like that both of my exes were present, but the reunion was nice despite the glitch. Tina splurged on catered food, a bartender, and a four-color banner. And she had a decent mix of old and new school hits leaking from her surround-sound speakers. The evening was pleasant until I felt a tap on my shoulder. I stopped chatting with two high school friends to see who'd interrupted. I turned around, praying it wasn't the ex I dumped via email.

Thankfully, Tina answered my prayers. "Angela," she said, "meet Jade. Jade, this is my sister."

My focus fell to their entangled fingers just as the mix rolled into a romantic ballad. Then I shifted my attention to Jade— the latest party arrival. Her lengthy hair was pulled back, placing emphasis on her toothy smile.

"Finally!" Jade said. "I would shake your hand, but a hug seems more appropriate." She stepped forward with open arms to embrace me. I was picky about hugging strangers, but I had to reciprocate.

I quickly withdrew my arm with an overwhelming desire to walk away.

"So?" Tina bumped her hip into mine. "Say something."

I hesitated. I couldn't say hello. It was too late for that. Nothing else came to mind. By the time I decided I could offer her something to drink, Momma stepped into our circle.

"Look at you," Momma said to Jade. "Sharp as always. You just left work?"

They chatted back and forth, catching up on this and that since their last conversation over dinner. After that tidbit of information, I didn't register another word. My eyes were glued to Tina, but she wouldn't look at me in return. So I stepped forward and grabbed her hand, forcing her to join me in the kitchen for a moment.

"Explain yourself," I demanded when we reached the back door.

"They just happened to meet. It wasn't like I arranged anything. Momma just popped up one day while we were standing

outside. You know she's a jack in a box. So, what do you think?"
I crossed arms and looked away.

"Angela?" she insisted.

I couldn't believe that Tina still expected me to overlook her
eight-month-long omission. And what exactly did she expect me
to say about girlfriend number three? I couldn't speak beyond the
obvious. Obviously, #3's firm physique fit nicely in her khakis
and polo shirt. Obviously, her minty scent was as pleasant as her
inviting smile. Obviously, she spoke intelligently. Obviously, my
sister wouldn't stay with a woman that undermined her happiness.

Aside from the obvious, I didn't like her. I wasn't feeling
her the second she thought it was okay to hug me. Now, how
could I tell Tina?

"I don't like her hair," I said.

Tina laughed and looked in #3's direction. "Momma nick-
named her Goldilocs."

Well…

Goldilocs was the director of her own developmental disabil-
ities agency. She had a staff of six; a clientele of eighty. Momma's
sister was included in the eighty. That was how Tina met Goldilocs. At first, she only wanted dyed tips, but a full cover looked
better. And she wanted to become a barber until life took her in
a different direction.

"Oh," I said, annoyed.

I knew Tina felt bad for excluding me because she started
to tell me even more random shit about Goldi that I didn't ask or
care about. I exhaled hard and stomped out the kitchen. I sat on
the couch as Tina made her way to the living room to whisper
in Goldi's ear. Then Goldi slowly chatted her way through our
crowd of guests to sit next to me.

"How does it feel to be back?" she asked.

"Fine," I said and stared at my new sandals. Everyone else
realized that I wanted to sit alone, but Goldi thought it was okay

come over and talk my ear off. Every word chipped away at the tolerance I needed to stay seated next to her.

"You know," she said, "once this federal grant comes through I'm hiring your sister."

I placed my eyes on hers for the second time that evening. The information was worth hearing.

"Once she's running the agency," Goldi added, "I can move on to other things. She's excited about it. She'll get to lead an organization without all the footwork."

"Really?" How the hell could Tina launch a business with me if she was busy tending to Goldilocs' responsibilities? "Well, ain't that something?"

...

Through twelve years of being out and about, dating and mating with too many fuck-ups and very little successes, I've experienced my share of stares, whispers, and flat-out disrespect from ex-girlfriends' family members. So, Tina's welcome back party is a partial victory. Her friends and family have embraced me from day one; our rapport is strengthened with each outing and conversation. But the prospect of establishing a decent connection with Tina's sister failed the minute she laid eyes on me.

"Your sister hates me," I say.

Tina laughs and steps out of her heels. "No, she doesn't." She pauses to slip off her red dress and toss it to the foot of her bed. "Baby, did you miss the label on her chest? She has a minimum three-month warming-up period."

Shit...

The warming-up never happens. Month after month, all I get is stank eye and slick attitude from Angela. For fifteen months, I've stayed patient and taciturn in her presence. I don't speak unless Angela speaks to me first, and our paths don't cross unless she steps into my space. I love Tina too much to spark friction between the dynamic duo. My relationship matters more than her sister's icy tongue or steel demeanor.

But Tina won't push her sister to act any differently— though she always remembers to umpire my interactions with Angela. "Listen," Tina says just before we step out of my car. "I just want to have a good time this evening. So *please* don't bring up anything about work."

Too bad my family lives fourteen hours away. If it weren't for the snowstorm up North, I'd spend the holiday with them. Tina better be glad I consider her mother a good substitute.

And Ms. Reid is hospitable as usual. She's plastered her home in red and gold and set her dining room table with fine dishes and candles and some knickknacks I can't name like we're dining at a five-star restaurant. Fourteen of us mix and mingle and play board games while teased by whiffs of sweet and savory foods.

When we eat, Ms. Reid takes special care to make my plate and grace me with seconds. After dinner, she shuffles us to the living room and surprises me with a gift.

"Wow," I say, running my fingers along a gold picture frame. When I opened my agency, I threw my first press article in a Dollar Tree frame. Ms. Reid has given my memento a suitable home; one with style, weight, and a matted interior.

"Momma," Tina says, "how in the world did you get that?"

"I took it from your office one day last week. I came by, but y'all weren't there."

I appreciate Ms. Reid's thoughtfulness, though I don't care for the extra attention. I'm aware that Tina's family stopped exchanging gifts years ago. She said they'd grown too old for presents. "My momma never got me anything I really wanted," she said. "And after my dad died, what was the point?"

Besides the unexpected gift, I also don't care for Angela's response. Her death stare is burning a hole in my chest. In her imagination, she's probably ripping my heart out right now. When I look over at her, she leaves the doorway and disappears to somewhere in the house. I'm sure she walked away pissed that she couldn't toss me into the fireplace to incinerate what's left.

"Thanks," I say to Ms. Reid. "This is sweet."

"Aw, wasn't much," she says and pats my leg.

I re-wrap the frame in the shimmering tissue paper and return it to the gift bag. I feel a little better in Angela's absence, but Tina senses my unease. I can't stop clenching my teeth or shifting my weight as we sit together on the loveseat.

"Now?" Tina whispers to me.

"Please," I mumble.

She garners her mother's attention and then announces to everyone, "I have something to tell y'all."

Shit…

The 'I' in her sentence isn't enough to keep everyone's eyes from moving from her face to mine. Eleven people stiffly wait, like Tina's words are the oil they need to move again— ready to blame me if she says something that falls short of their approval.

"We're engaged," Tina shouts with spirit fingers.

The instant smiles and pour of congratulations curb my anxiety. Ms. Reid springs forward and wraps her arms around Tina. The moment couldn't have been more perfect. Her family is genuinely happy for our pledged union. The only outlier is Angela.

She walks back into the family room as soon as her mother wipes lipstick from my cheek. Angela approaches with a shy grin and says, "Did I hear my sister correctly?"

Before I can speak, Tina steps beside me, prepared to navigate our interaction. "You did," Tina answers.

"Dang," Angela says, "too bad there's no champagne. You're a great addition to this family. We need someone to shake things up a bit around here." She adds a little zest to her vote of support by playfully pushing my arm. "So, will there be a wedding?"

And with that question Tina morphs into a future bride—laying out plans for a ceremony and reception *we* haven't decided to have yet.

We sit down together so they can talk comfortably. I keep my mouth closed to allocate focus and energy to my intuitive senses. The setting is right. The timing is right. But everything about Angela is entirely wrong.

Who is she fooling? No amount of smiles, questions, or wedding suggestions will allow me to believe she's abandoned ship so easily. The mask she's wearing is attractive and convincing, but it reeks of manipulation. Only a fool in love would let Tina fall for another second of Angela's bullshit reaction.

"Baby," I say to interrupt them. "I know how badly you wanted to do this today, but maybe we made a mistake. Are we ready for this? We shouldn't have—"

"Jade, what the hell?" Tina says. Her eyes jump around the room to ensure no one else has tuned into the conversation. To minimize the risk, she pulls me from the loveseat and toward the hallway, a few steps away from the front door for privacy. I try to comfort her, bring her into my arms so that I can explain. She pushes my arms away and I try again, pinning my hands on her hips to keep her close. Eventually, she settles into my chest to avoid a scene.

While I have the chance, I kiss her forehead once. Then I drop my mouth to her ear. "I'm sorry," I whisper, "but I won't let your sister do that to you." I stroke the small of Tina's back, hoping she'll remain calm enough to lend her patience.

She lifts her face to mine. "What do you mean?"

"Look at her. She hasn't said one word. Not one word in your defense. A minute ago she was picking out our colors and suggesting honeymoon destinations. Now she's sitting there like she doesn't know what's happening... How fucking convenient."

Tina slowly turns her head toward Angela. Her sister is engaging in conversation with a cousin. Her glances, however, take frequent trips in our direction.

Tina looks at me with sadness and confusion. "I'm not going anywhere, baby," I say. "But she's got a problem. A problem called the epitome of jealousy."

Shit...

The problem with calling her sister out is the danger of insinuation. I don't want Tina to assume I'm calling her sister insane. I also don't want her to feel like I'm pushing her toward an ultimatum. When Tina drops her forehead on my chest, I feel as manipulative as Angela for pretending like I regretted our engagement— but I had to do something. I hope this moment of silence will help Tina forgive my behavior and words.

"Tina?" I desperately need her to say something, to give me some indication of her thoughts.

She lifts her head and grasps my arms. "Now you see why I waited."

Who Cooks For You?
Claudia Moss

The day favored a cloudy crystal. Staring into it behind seashell curtains at the cottage window, Mara had an uninterrupted view of the beach. Yards away, seagulls chased something a small knot of children tossed gleefully. A couple held hands as they strolled under a whimsical sky, and incoming tides lent the ocean a surreal beauty, the waves unhurried, not choppy like yesterday. Mara stepped closer to the window. A familiar figure slowly making its way toward the cottage claimed her attention. The closer it got, the clearer Mara could see how the scene paled in comparison to her mate of five years.

Her swag hella sexy, Kerri Watson stopped a short distance from the sandy walk leading to their cottage. Mara watched as her woman looked out to sea and then shifted her attention to the playing children, swimmers, and the outline of hotel properties colorful against the skyline. A strange feeling flushed through her, and Mara suddenly felt as if she were seeing their relationship clearly for the first time since they'd arrived. Then, as though overwhelmed by the same sensation, Kerri Watson began making a show of outrunning the incoming waves.

WHO COOKS FOR YOU?

Mara peered at her. Kerri was the epitome of spontaneity. Mara loved that about her, although she hated that Kerri frowned on anything Mara didn't tell her first. Having moved that way for years, it still irked Mara that Kerri never reciprocated. But Mara knew Kerri wasn't wholly to blame. Mara was her own problem. She nursed a persistent fear of letting go. Of anyone or anything. For instance, Mara might have stopped studying Kerri from behind the seashell curtains to do something she enjoyed or run outside to join her playing in the sand, but she didn't. She was stuck. Plain and simple. Caught in a bubble she had no words to burst.

Right now, something inside softly insisted she remain where she was. Earlier that morning, Kerri had questioned Mara about her evening plans, thinking Mara would be on the cottage deck, reading. And Mara's constant pattern had given her room to think little else. If she didn't venture outside with Kerri, she didn't leave the cottage at all. Only reached for one of the books she'd packed or pressed the on button to light her Kindle Fire.

Mara's brows crinkled, her thoughts heated kernels.

If Kerri's desire was to enjoy their vacation alone, then why invite her on a getaway for a week on Hapuna Beach, their favorite Big Island paradise known for its picturesque white beaches? Or was it Kerri's favorite? Mara had stopped knowing much of anything about her favorites years ago. Empty had become her middle name.

Until now.

She rubbed a forefinger across one eye and blinked. A brown-skinned woman with a sensual stroll and wide hips and an explosion of kinky curls seductively made her way across the blonde sand. Mara studied her, mesmerized. The woman moved as though she were dancing, her confidence intoxicating. Gliding, she strolled like… like she was heading straight for Kerri. Mara squinted. No, she couldn't be. Not in front of their cottage. Yet the smiling beauty, skin glistening, body eye-popping sexy in an orange-red

bikini and matching knee-length, sheer wrap, continued sashaying. The wrap fell open as she walked, exposing thick thighs.
Stunning, the fabric, tied low under a jeweled navel, showed off
a flat waist and flawless skin. Mara couldn't blink even as the
vixen made a beeline to Kerri.

Mara wanted to curse.

Feet immobile, she bit her lips, batted her eyelashes, and
fought the urge to scream. Why was Kerri so striking in baggy
white linen shorts and white T? Luscious locks twisted back off
of her beautiful face made her more appealing.

Stiff, Mara knew it was coming.

As if the stranger could feel Mara watching and needing to
see what she was about to witness, the vixen refused to disap-
point. Stopping inches from Mara's woman, the stranger leaned
into Kerri's firefighter arms, steadying herself using Kerri's waist,
and puckered her lips. Kerri accepted her kiss as if she had been
doing so a lifetime… as if the ocean were an interloper on their
intimacy… and as if the vixen were summoned expressly to help
Kerri show Mara just how over their relationship was.

Mara's throat tightened. But there was no looking away.

At that moment, Mara trembled, the dam overflowing within
her heart. One hand covered her mouth. Violated, she tiptoed
through the cottage to the master bedroom and reclined on the
king-sized bed, the sea-green comforter a consoling caress. She
closed wet eyes and, even though she felt hard-pressed to remember in the cold sunlight, she willed herself to sleep to forget the
last time she'd savored Kerri's kisses.

...

"Hey, lady. Why so sad?"

Mara jumped, shifting in the deck chair on the patio of the
Ocean Terrace Restaurant. Earlier, she'd awaken from a restorative

sleep in the quiet of the cottage when Kerri hadn't returned. In a cold shower, she'd decided not to sit in shadows, waiting and pining. Instead, she conditioned her braids with cholesterol, draped a pinkish-purple, rhinestone-studded sarong about her curves, grabbed her key card and walked into a warm Hawaiian night.

"Oh, hi," she greeted, coming back from the maze of her thoughts. "Is it that obvious?"

"If I didn't know better, I'd think the sky had fallen, and you and Chicken Little lost your best friend in the catastrophe." A symphony of laughter muted the noisy chatter of nearby tables of Hapuna Beach diners.

Mara laughed, looking around for the owner of the flirty voice and laughter. She spied a woman resting against a deck column, arms folded and dressed in a chef's sparkling white jacket. Hmmm. She hadn't allowed herself to look at another woman in a long time. Least of all a white one. Looking at other women led to jealous outbursts and erratic conversations in which Kerri accused her of cheating and reminded her that if she ever got wind of it, Mara was history.

But things had changed. An alluring swag about this woman spelled exquisite. Mara felt a twinge below her belly button. Fine described her well. Tall, dark-haired, armed with an arresting smile and intoxicating confidence, the woman's attention to Mara's presence buttonholed any notion of what Kerri was doing with Miss Hawaii somewhere on the island.

"Don't know about Chicken Little, but in a very real sense, I have."

"Hopefully he didn't leave with your appetite?"

"She."

"When you least expect it, that ocean leaves you all sorts of treasures. Who would've guessed she'd treat me to a real-live mermaid this evening? Talk about being glad I woke up. So you know, I'm accepting applications for a prime position." Undeniable charm lit her face. "Interested?"

Mara smirked and then surprised herself, flashing her long-forgotten, Miss Miami smile, once reserved for bringing attractive butches to her side in pre-Kerri Watson years. Right now, she felt alive, charged. Every cell in her body vibrated. The woman was flirting. And was doing it so well, Mara found herself tottering. An old way of being loosened inside her, slipping away like a yellow silk ribbon unraveling on the breeze.

"That depends."

"On what? You don't need anyone's approval to apply, do you?"

The directness stymied Mara, made her explore her options. So she took her time responding, while the chef read her face.

"I wouldn't be sitting here if I did."

The woman grinned. "Bet you haven't been spontaneous in years. When was the last time you spoke to a stranger in a restaurant? Better yet, do you dine by choice or neglect?"

The sexy chef crossed the short distance from the column to Mara's table, one hand extended. Mara could see her eyes were blue drops on a white canvas.

"Bonjour, Belle. Nous n'avons pas rencontré officiellement. Mon nom est Michaela Cartier. Comment êtesvous?"

Slowly, Mara accepted the hand, the nails short and unpainted. The instant their flesh met, warmth flooded Mara's skin and left her glistening. "I'm wonderful. Nice to meet you. I'm Mara."

"Mon plaisir, Mademoiselle Mara. S'il vous plaît appelez-moi Cartier."

The language music to her ears, it sent another fiery current from Mara's breasts to her belly and beyond. Mara's thighs clenched, and she casually jumped her legs under the soft fabric of her sarong to thwart the reaction.

But Cartier noticed. The purple breath of Mara's beachwear

against her skin dead bolted Cartier's gaze to the stunning, cur-
vaceous woman.

"Cartier," Mara repeated, marveling at her ability to speak
under the jarring attraction she was feeling. In grad school, French
was at home in her mouth; well enough, even, to relish a summer
on the French Riviera with—. Mara spit her then ex's name from
her tongue before it conjured images of her arrogant phantom and
returned her attention to this Michaela Cartier.

A gentlewoman with electric eyes, Cartier nodded at the seat
in front of Mara's table. Her smile hiked rakishly as she straddled
the chair. Under the patio's muted lights, Mara gave herself permission to skirt the other woman's disturbingly handsome face
and curly, chestnut hair. Mara hadn't been this moved in a long,
dry season. She shifted. Yesterday, if someone had prophesied
she'd be hypnotized looking in a white woman's eyes, Mara
might have frowned.

"Are you fluent?"

"Are you ravishing?"

"How long have you lived on the island?"

"How long will you be right here?"

"Do you have family here?"

"Do you intend to let your ex think she runs Miss Mara?"

"My ex?"

"Are you not here… alone?"

Mara feigned annoyance. Though adorable, Cartier's touché
was beginning to work her nerves. "Do you often answer a question with a question?" Mara shifted for the tenth time.

"Only when my queries go unanswered, yes." Cartier grinned
and pushed back in the chair. She stretched her legs under the
table, looking at Mara playfully. When the tips of her shoes grazed
Mara's sandaled feet, a clenching sensation in Mara's thighs returned, setting off a quiet riot deep in her honeywell, drawing her
upright. Embarrassed, Mara averted her eyes.

Despite a similar bolt pinning her to her chair, Cartier registered Mara's reaction coolly.

Mara hoped this debonair woman didn't think she behaved like one of the great green sea turtles she'd seen sunbathing in the Hapuna Beach State Park. Slow and unfazed. She really didn't know how to flirt anymore but she didn't want to come off as a neglected woman out on a mission impossible, so she breathed deeply and straightened her back, lifting her breasts. Truth was the best tonic.

"Okay, you're right. I haven't entertained a stranger anywhere in a long time."

Cartier nodded. "Embedded in that, I gather, is a no to spontaneity, *oui*?"

Mara said nothing.

Smiling, Cartier tossed a lifeline. Mara had caught it at the sound of "Hey, lady," but she willed herself to maintain the woman's stare, exhaling slowly. The women smiled, their brown and blue gazes taking in the nuances of the other's breathing. They imagined many things; one touching the other's skin, and two, wondering how enjoyable a stroll together on a night beach would be.

Excited yet hesitant, Mara didn't know what the night would hold, but whoever did?

...

The drive north up the Kohala Coast blazed with raw Hawaiian beauty, same as Mara's host. At times silent then talkative, Cartier handled the Jeep with a smooth dexterity, no speeding to exhibit her prowess and prosperity; merely, she was a woman aware of herself and the feelings of others. Though Mara had never allowed a stranger she'd known a few hours to take her anywhere, she felt safe beside this unassumingly appealing chef.

Pink streaks stained the horizon. Under it, a shadowy ocean and long, lonely beach raced for miles. Mara was grateful for the whispering wind as they whizzed through the evening. Listening to it canceled a need for small talk. When the Jeep eventually pulled into a gated, guarded community and came to a stop before a palatial estate with a circular drive, the bottom dropped out of Mara's silence.

On the lawn, a bevy of fowl honked, strutting as if hunting a new nesting spot.

"Ducks. How cute! They remind me of the ones on your nature preserves."

"For good reason. They're one in the same, the Nene or Hawaiian Geese. They used to be endangered; now they're protected, and so much so, these guys are beyond the law, free to do whatever they please, including fertilize my lawn daily."

Mara couldn't resist teasing Cartier. "Your gratitude is apparent. Lucky you."

"Yes, I'm blessed in many ways." Looking from Mara to the night sky, Cartier murmured softly, "The heavens match your wrap." When Mara smiled, Cartier added, "For the record, you are more beautiful than any sunset I've ever seen, and I've been all over the world."

"That's kind of you. *Merci.*"

Cartier took Mara's hand on the short walk to her front door. Mara trembled, a baby bird on the grass under its nest, even after she and Cartier had strolled hand in hand earlier along the beach.

"It's okay. If it'll make you feel better, you can call my manager. I want you to be comfortable. Your hesitancy, I understand. After all, I'm a stranger... inviting you into her home... after nightfall. Jolene will tell you I'm some of the safest company on the island." Cartier flashed a spellbinding smile. "And no, I've never dated her."

Mara inhaled, willing herself to swallow her jitters and be a woman. Actually, Mara liked her and the way she took care not to wrinkle her sarong, and the scent of her skin and the feel of her embrace when she'd helped Mara out of the Jeep.

"I'm okay, thanks. It's just that I'm… more hungry than anything."

"Come on. You really thought I didn't know. Girl, I heard you trying to loud talk your stomach on our stroll, thus, the invite to my humble abode. But don't worry, though. I've got the perfect feast."

"And what would that be, Chef Cartier?" They were climbing lighted, circular steps to impressive double doors.

"An immovable feast."

"Like Hemingway's novel?" Mara's giggles ruffled the evening breeze.

Cartier glanced at her, brows raised, pleasantly surprised. "*Oui.* Something like that." She couldn't help it. She had always admired an intelligent, beautiful woman, and this one didn't seem to know she had her and the Big Island on a string.

A sexy saxophone and crisp air greeted them when Cartier opened the doors to a foyer without end. Mara was transfixed. She admired the openness of the house, which allowed her to appreciate everything: artfully arranged antiques, posh furnishings, Oriental rugs, Indian and African masks, and vases that left her jaw agape. On the walls were sensual paintings of lovers or beautiful women. In spite of the room's affluence, though, a simple elegance reigned.

"Like it?"

"Trick question, eh? It's immaculate." Mara slipped out of her sandals and wiggled her toes on the cool hardwood. "Whoever that is on the sax is about to make me weep. I love the sound of a horn, be it a saxophone, trombone, or trumpet. Mmm."

"*Merci beaucoup.* That's one of my friends in the music industry. David Cochrane. Whenever he visits the island, he dines at the restaurant."

"Is he one of the artists in the celebrity photos on the walls in your place?"

Cartier nodded. "If you like, when you leave, I'll gift you with all of his CDs. They're priceless... like you."

She started to say thank you, but Michaela Cartier's mouth was dangerously close to hers. A soft weakening was already happening in her knees and her arms reacted. Swinging nervously, they fluttered and wrapped her body, her hands also lost, smoothing her sarong and raking her braids. Turning away from the intense woman, Mara marveled at the beauty of an ornate mirror. That's when Cartier reached out and touched her braids. In the huge, oval frame, Cartier's stare penetrated her, daring her to look away. When Mara didn't, lava erupted within her, seeping volcanic heat over her shoulders and breasts. Cartier could feel the eruption; she was standing that close. Saw it on her quivering lips. But she didn't want to incinerate Mara just yet. What she had in mind was going to take all night, perhaps all week, and hopefully, all month. But first, she had to satiate Mara's hunger, before she extinguished a flame flushing beads of sweat across Mara's forehead. A patient lover, Cartier knew an inferno's notoriety hovered on how well she fanned a woman's hunger.

"Get acquainted with the place, Miss Mara. There are no pets, outside of the ones on the lawn." Cartier chuckled. "I'll set the table on the second-floor patio. Let's see... when you hear Dave sing "Yellow Bird"— my favorite— head this way. *Oui, amour?*"

Mara agreed with a tilt of her head. Cartier's next question scattered rose petals at her feet. "Who cooks for you?"

"No one." Mara didn't bother with lies. "I cook for me."

"Have you ever asked or allowed anyone to cook for you?"

Mara didn't answer, only smiled and strolled through a doorway behind her.

Cartier's humming trailed her into a day room, of a sort, down the hall from the kitchen. Amber and sparkling. From there, she drifted throughout the mansion, admiring Cartier's eclectic taste in colors and patterns and fixtures. Upstairs, on the third level, she floated into one of the bedrooms, where, in the mirrors, she might've been Daisy weeping over The Great Gatsby's opulent, pastel shirts. In the reading room off of the bedroom, she peered out of a high window and noticed the landscaping and the pool below were enchanting, softly lit worlds.

Before she could marvel too long, she realized the music was piped throughout the house, and she needn't worry about missing Cartier's signature song.

Mara observed and drifted. Admired and wandered.

There was so much to see. And not one bit of evidence or picture of another woman. Mara was enthralled anew. Then there it was, seemingly within the hour. Tender kisses on her earlobes. The saxophonist was singing about a yellow bird soaring across the sky, flying free. Unforgettable, the voice, the music, and the aroma of spicy food guided her back to the patio, where Cartier had set a cherry-wood table with over-sized, lavender-scented candles, colorful platters of food, and two goblets of red wine.

"Come. Sit beside me." Cartier offered her a steamy white hand towel. While Mara cleaned up, Cartier couldn't stop herself from stroking Mara's braids. Treating the back of her hand to the silkiness of Mara's cheek, she softly admitted, "Something tells me you're not a finicky female with persnickety taste buds. Thank God!" Her laugh cozy, Mara became a stream seeking her river.

A stack of pearly-white plates called Mara. "That something told you correctly. I'm a hungry female, thank you!"

"I hoped you'd say that." Cartier reached for Mara's hand. She paused to appreciate the pink manicure before bringing a sushi roll to Mara's lips. "Eel, salmon, and cream cheese. Made it myself."

At first, Mara frowned. The last time someone fed her, she

was sick, ten-years-old, at Grandma Honey's and out of school for two days. Yet… she'd often dreamed of Kerri feeding her. Once upon a time.

"A dollar for your thoughts."

Mara laughed, looking around. "I like that. Dollar thoughts."

"All day."

Mara reached for the sushi roll from Cartier's hand. "Thanks."

"No. Try letting go, baby. I don't question my inner woman. I allow her to manifest my dreams. Bow to your inner lady, and give the universe your reins. Allowance is sweet."

Mara parted her lips and permitted Cartier to feed her.

Mercy… was it luscious! From the Asian soups, creamy mashed potatoes to roasted garlic lamb chops. She hummed under the savory flavors. Her tongue curled around lime and pumpkin seed-sprinkled salad. Charred salmon topped with watercress and braised beans. If she never tasted paradise again, she'd forever have this night.

"Oh, God, Cartier, why all this food?" She had to moan. "I hope you're not expecting me to eat everything." Mara moaned like her baby cousin used to moan when she served him sliced hotdogs drenched in ketchup. Her lashes fanned her cheeks in reverence. "This is unbelievable. Thank you." She could barely speak, squeezing the words out around blissful chewing.

"Reserve all praise until the meal's end, please."

Mara laughed and rolled her eyes, scrunching her lips in feigned annoyance.

Smiling, Cartier speared a bit of shrimp salad dripping with mango basil vinaigrette and gently placed it on Mara's tongue. She followed that with forkfuls of herb-crusted sweet peas. The seared ahi tuna made Mara conjure speaking in tongues. A wave of fireworks burst in her mouth and bolted to her stomach and sent euphoria throughout her body, sating her in tides of spicy satisfaction. But when Mara's chewing slowed and grape seed oil slicked her lips and Cartier's tongue groaned with a desire to taste Mara, Cartier leaned into the smaller woman. The intoxication of the chef's cologne quieted Mara's Kerri-laced thoughts.

"What's to drink?"

"My love juice."

"After this meal, I don't think I'll need alco—"

Cartier's moist lips on her shoulder wiped the word from the air. The kiss so tender, it closed her eyes. "I promise not to abuse the gift of your reins. *Bon?*"

Mara looked at the woman and lifted her chin. "*Bon.*"

That understood, Cartier presented her with a flask of blended rum, fresh pineapple, and orange slices. The rum's scrumptious smell raced Mara's blood before she swallowed.

"Oh my goodness, this is heaven. I think I had something that was supposed to be this in a restaurant a few days ago. It's tangy. Tropical."

"Delighted you like it." Cartier buried her nose in Mara's hair. Mara watched from her peripheral vision. The blue eyes were closed. Mara wondered if Cartier felt the same surge of electricity that coursed through her. "No apologies. By now you know I'm powerless to not inhale you. Dessert?"

"Maybe later. My taste buds are still enamored with dinner."

"Superb. While I clean up, would you care to freshen up before dessert? I took the liberty of leaving toiletries and one of Mother's never-worn sarongs on the guest bed. She comes to get away from her *jolie vie parisienne* about four times a year. Is that good?"

"*Oui* and *merci.* You must tell me all about her pretty Parisian life one day." Mara's playful tone bowed to compassion. "But wait. Aren't you hungry? Or are you the sort of chef who eats as she cooks?" She glanced at Cartier's slim waist and toned arms and deduced the woman did not lack for anything, least of all food and exercise.

"I am a dessert woman."

"I've always loved sweets, so I know what you mean."

Cartier doubted that. "Mango puree with a dash of lime is my fav."

Mara's initial impulse was a resounding, "Not!" But when Cartier washed her hands and dipped one finger in a bowl of mango puree, put her finger in Mara's mouth and Mara licked the tangy finger clean, Mara changed her mind. Even had her wondering how long Cartier's clean-up chores would take on her way upstairs.

Not long afterwards, Mara was spread lengthwise across cherry wood, between huge candles. Whiffs of lavender from her hair and bath and scented candles mingled with the salty ocean spray lacing the evening air wafting through the patio screens.

Cartier towered above her. Softly, sensually, she untied the new sarong and gently removed the gold fabric from Mara's body. The woman was enthralling. Cartier stared, careful not to miss a single detail. Long deep breaths steadied her, while her blue eyes slowly traipsed the flawless brown flesh under her fingertips.

Now the saxophonist was performing "Cocoa Butter." Mara felt the words in her pores, wanting, as she did, this woman under her skin like cocoa butter.

Cartier dipped her fingers into a tiny glass pot and dripped mango puree over Mara's breasts. She relished the firm globes under her palms. This, she thought, was paradise. She drizzled the delicious-smelling puree down Mara's quivering belly and watched it pool in the crevice of her navel. She noted Mara's quivers and jarred breathing when she lowered her head to the fruit-laced flesh.

One supple thigh crossed the other in the need to conceal her pussy from this suddenly foreign woman. Tumbling out of the moment, Mara felt naked, blatantly nude. Her palms shot up to conceal her shy nipples, and then slowly, they remembered, changed their mind and pushed down on the table.

Aware of the shift, Cartier leaned over Mara and, kissing her face and neck, gently slipped her tongue into Mara's mouth. She prayed for an endless night. Fascinated, Cartier hadn't met a woman who claimed her breath in years, and her hands knew this, delighted as they were at the texture of Mara's thighs, waist, and hips. "You're perfection. Simply gorgeous." Her lips and hands worshiped Mara, and under their attentive stroking, Mara's long, lean thighs parted. Heat hummed under her skin, electricity sparking wherever Cartier touched her. Especially when her hand caressed the dark downy curls of Mara's pussy and then, one finger at a time, until there were four inside Mara, Cartier pressed her silky petals, pushing and pumping rhythmically, causing Mara to grip the table's edge. When Mara's back arched, inviting Cartier closer, Cartier's mouth seared Mara's aromatic flesh. Her pussy wept with pleasure, moaning Michaela's name. Cartier slathered her in hot, moist kisses, rocking her, thrilling her, and skillfully owning an explosion that began as tremors in Mara's thighs.

Mara's body screamed for joy. And released. Sweat-drenched, she embraced the broad, lightly freckled back, breathing softly, while Cartier's silky chestnut curls spilled fragrantly over her face. Neither spoke for a long time.

Finally, Cartier broke the silence. "You good?" She lifted herself from the brown woman's body and massaged Mara's feet, until she brought leisurely sighs from Mara's parted lips. "Seconds?"

Mara answered with a slightly raised toe.

Cartier understood, kissing it. She was captivated at its sweet, salty flavor. Soft, well-manicured feet with a ringed toe or two did it for her. In Cartier's ravenous mouth, Mara's toes quivered, her legs jerking sporadically. Mara's nails streaked grids the length of Cartier's biceps. But Cartier didn't seem to notice. With her kisses tattooing Mara's ankle, then traveling up her shapely calf and branding her inner thigh, the pungent aroma of Mara's pussy showered Cartier's senses with more pleasure.

Sitting not to miss a drop of her mouth-watering affair, Cartier trickled mango puree across Mara's exposed passion flower. The need to taste Mara again surged through her. She lowered her head, plunging into Mara's saccharine flow. With Mara's fingers deep in chestnut curls, Cartier's tongue lavished Mara's bud with wet strokes; the mango mixed with Mara's candied juice coated Cartier's tongue in a savory fruitiness. Cartier lifted her and widened the space between the moaning woman's thighs. This time Cartier closed her eyes and moaned. The woman tasted delectable; Cartier's moans became groans and slipped into sighs. Mercy, mercy, mercy! Her tongue laved Mara's clit and then slicked her petals until Mara's moans commingled with hers on the ocean-scented breezes drifting through the patio screen.

Of all the women Cartier had ever known, she had no memory of a woman quite as satisfying.

And Mara complained and kicked and wiggled and cried out under Cartier's sultry lovemaking. She screamed louder when Cartier's fingers entered her own mouth, picked up a momentum, and then disappeared inside Mara forcefully, possessively, faster, slower, then deeper, until Mara bucked and held onto Cartier's broad shoulders to keep from evaporating into thin air.

Every so often, Cartier inhaled and made certain Mara was still breathing.

Meanwhile, Mara fought to gather herself. And not shake so hard until delicate dessert dishes found their way to the kitchen tiles.

Yesterday, mango had been Cartier's all-time favorite dessert. Yet tonight, the piquant fruit lost its sweetness next to this woman, this Mara from Miami. Everything about her set Cartier on notice, from her amber-flecked eyes, to that softly rounded face, those full, sugarsweet lips, the charming voice, her quiet wit, her caring demeanor, and that voluptuous body. Kissing Mara topped sipping expensive, aged, aromatic wine, while other parts of her possessed the power to make Cartier relocate, give up, give in, and cook. She'd already reconciled with the undisputed fact of love at first sight, but damn! This moment was an oasis in the falling flakes of a gypsy's crystal ball.

"Is that CD on repeat?"

Cartier ignored the question. She scooped Mara from the monstrous wooden island and settled her in the center of her apron-tied lap.

"If you're tired of it, I'll pull up anything you want to hear. Just say the word."

"Oh, mercy," Mara teased, kissing Cartier's cheek. "You didn't answer with a question." She crossed long legs and placed her right hand on Cartier's forehead. "You okay?"

Cartier laughed and pulled Mara into her chest, inhaling deep whiffs of the woman and walking her fingers up Mara's damp thigh. "Nah. I've got a case of the Mara bug, and damn..." She shook chestnut curls from her eyes. "I don't even know your full name."

"No complaints about the CD. I love it, since it's all I've heard." Mara laughed. "I was just asking." She smiled. "My name is Mara Ann Reagan, and I like you, Michaela."

"The pleasure is solely mine, Miss Reagan. I like you more. And you can call me Michaela, which no one else dares do, or dog catcher, for that matter. For you, I'll always answer." Cartier licked puree from the tip of Mara's nose and then smooched her cheek and neck. Mara fell backward, laughing. "I'm blessed to have met you."

"And me you, Michaela. Your name is lovely. Why don't you like it?"

"Never said I didn't like it."

"Right." Mara rolled brown eyes. "Yeah, well, I never imagined I'd be attracted to… and do what I've done and so fast… with anyone… especially not with a white girl."

"Is that so? I'm glad you listen to your life. Isn't that what Oprah says?"

Mara kissed her finger and tapped Cartier's nose. "Amongst others."

"Had you not gotten dressed after seeing your ex cavorting in front of your cottage and brought your sexy self to my restaurant, well, who knows how long it would've taken us to find one another? Hell, I don't know when I'd have flown into Miami and bumped into you." She grinned mischievously. "*Vous me comprenez?*"

Mara nodded. "*Oui.*" She was determined to flap dust from her wavering, self-conscious French. "*Vous m'aider avec mon Français?*"

Cartier pulled Mara into her body and rocked her back and forth like her grandmother had done years ago, when she visited her on school holidays and they laughed about Mara being little, so little that her feet couldn't reach the floor. Mara closed her eyes. A feeling of complete and utter delight flooded her body. She became perfectly motionless.

"Woman, I will help you with your French and anything, and I do mean anything, else. For starters, I'll go with you to Watson's cottage later today to retrieve your belongings. And if the kind lady has done away with whatever, I'll replace everything. With time, laughter, good food, and Anita Baker's good love, she will be history. No harsh words or wishes."

"What do you know about Anita Baker?"

"The same thing you know about the French Riviera."

Cartier flicked a braid off Mara's shoulder. "Remember. No harshness. We can't receive our blessings that way."

"So what are you now… a spiritual chef?"

"*J'aime ça!* I like that. *Merci.*"

"*De rien.*" Mara's face broke into a smiling sunrise. More bits of the forgotten language resurfaced. She straddled Cartier, placing her fingers into curls along the woman's temples and gently lifting hair away from her face. "What do you say Chef Michaela about what my said exgirlfriend could be feeling now? If, let's say, she's worried about where I am."

Cartier looked at her thoughtfully, oblivious to how peeved she'd always been when other women slipped uninvited fingers into her hair or referenced their ex. "I say she's feeling what she's supposed to be feeling right about now. And I commend her. She brought you on a Hawaiian getaway to get away, and I found you." She winked and brought warm lips to Mara's neck, causing the smaller woman to open her mouth and giggle.

"That distraction will not earn you cool points." Mara pinched Cartier's nose. Baring her teeth, Cartier left love bites across her naked shoulder.

"You worried about her? If you are, I'll take you there. No biggie."

Mara shook her head. "No way, no how. I'm glad I left my cell to—"

"—Be in the moment," Cartier finished. "With it, you might've been sitting in the restaurant focused on whether you should text or call her. So yes, everything works out." Cartier gave her a devilish grin. "Well, what would you like to do now, Miss Mara?"

"Check out your movie collection and change that damn CD."

Cartier nodded. "I can handle that. You don't ask for much." She smirked. "At least... not for now. As for the movie, you can have at it. I'll be sleep soon. Me. I don't prefer anything mechanical watching me while I sleep. I saw *The Exorcist.* The TV is set to a timer, so I'll show you to the remote."

They both laughed. Then Cartier's tone changed and her forefinger and thumb brought Mara's chin inches from her kiss.

WHO COOKS FOR YOU?

"I realize this could be considered premature," the French woman began hesitantly, "but may I cook for you for the remainder of your stay on the Big Island? *Oui*? We can talk about what you've got going in Miami in the event you want to explore options." She studied Mara's play exasperation, her pleading brows lifted. "Wait. Before you get started, I haven't demonstrated my full array of culinary prowess yet."

She wouldn't need much convincing. Mara shook her braids, laughed, and hugged Cartier's neck. "Only if I can be your menu's main dessert."

"Deal." Cartier laughed, smothering her in kisses. "If I'd known it was going to be this easy to negotiate the arrangement, I'd have started with dessert and worked backward."

Mara rested her head in the crook of Cartier's neck. "Can you carry me upstairs, Michaela?"

"No, ma'am." Cartier playfully set Mara on her bare feet and grabbed her right hand. "How will I be in rare form to retrieve your belongings in a few hours, if my back is out of whack from throwing you up all night and then carrying you up flights of stairs? You'll make that a habit." She laughed and made a pretense of looking Mara up and down. "And you just ate, too."

"So much for I will do *anything* for you, Miss Mara."

Cartier just laughed, dimming the lights before leading Mara from the kitchen.

Contributing Writers

S. Andrea Allen is a native southerner and out Black lesbian writer, scholar, educator, and founder of BLF Press, an indie publisher dedicated to amplifying the work of women of color. Her works in progress include *A Failure to Communicate,* a collection of short fiction (2016), and a collection of creative non-fiction and essays.

Stephanie's day jobs include teaching writing and literature to college students and running BLF Press. She loves to travel and spends a good deal of her time on the road with GiGi her gray sedan, or barreling through the air in a metal tube. Most nights you can find her snuggled up on the couch with Mango, her feline muse and road cat.

Jai Allis writes for pleasure (and sanity) on a not-so-daily basis. Jai looks forward to completing her current writing projects, which (upon completion) will result in a spiral-bound publishing guide for independent authors, a story featuring a black lesbian couple who happen to be sole survivors in a post-apocalyptic world, and a short story collection with socio-political themes. Jai is a Memphis, TN native with aspirations to travel the world. In the meantime, she's headed back to school to spin a social work degree into sex therapy.

Lauren Cherelle uses her time and talents to traverse imaginary and professional worlds. She manages and writes for Resolute Publishing, an indie publisher that helps transforms dreams into realities for female writers. Her second novel, *The Dawn of Nia*— a story about the sting of abandonment, the difficulty of forgiveness, and the grace of transformative love— will be released in the spring of 2016. Her short story "A Secret Validation" was published in *G.R.I.T.S: Girls Raised in the South: An Anthology of Queer Womyn's Voices & Their Allies* (2013).

During the week, Lauren works in nonprofit development and administration. On weekends, she hangs up her fundraising hat to focus on developmental editing, graphic design projects, and personal writing. She resides in Louisville, KY with her partner of twelve years. Together, they aspire to open a business incubator that houses a community-based mental wellness center that serves women and families.

Outside of reading, writing, and working, Lauren volunteers as a child advocate. She loves to visit new cities, binge watch her favorite shows, play in her curly hair, and teach women to explore and adore the power of intimacy.

Sheree L. Greer is a Milwaukee native and currently hosts Oral Fixation, the only LGBTQ Open Mic series in Tampa Bay, teaches writing and literature at St. Petersburg College, and founded The Kitchen Table Literary Arts Center to showcase and support the work of ancestor, elder, and contemporary women writers of color. Her debut novel, *Let the Lover Be* is available from

Bold Strokes Books. Learn more about Sheree and her work at www.shereelgreer.com.

La Toya Hankins is the author of *SBF Seeking* and *K-Rho: The Sweet Taste of Sisterhood*. She is a native of North Carolina and currently resides in Durham, NC. She is an East Carolina University graduate who earned her Bachelor of Arts degree in journalism with a minor in political science. During her college career, she became a member of Zeta Phi Beta Sorority, Inc. Lambda Mu chapter. She currently serves as the president of her sorority's Chapel Hill, NC graduate chapter.

Hankins enjoys reading and writing fiction. She is a co-founder and currently serves as the chair of Shades of Pride, a LGBT organization that hosts a yearly event in the Triangle area. SOP's mission is to create opportunities to acknowledge and celebrate the diversity of North Carolina's LGBTQ communities. She is the proud pet parent of a 12-year-old terrier named Neo. Hankins considers writer and fellow Zeta Phi Beta Sorority, Inc. member Zora Neale Hurston as her role model for her ability to capture the essence of the African American Southern experience and living the motto, "I don't weep at the world, I'm am too busy sharpening my oyster knife."

Faith Mosley is a 48-year-old, Black, butch, dyke scratching out a living in the high desert of New Mexico.

Eternity Philops began her formal writing career with her college newspaper. Her most significant piece was her public coming out as a Black lesbian, an essay rebutting attacks on the campus LGBT organization. Widely received, Eternity soon found herself openly sharing her literary gift. Her writings have been featured in a number of Black lesbian publications including *Kuma* and

Gay Black Female Magazine. She was also a contributing writer to the online periodicals of *SABLE Magazine*, which focused on matters concerning lesbians of color, and *The NUBIANO Project*, a Black community news site.

After creating her own independent publishing company, Black Tygre Publications, Eternity released her debut title in 2008, *Visions of a Cryptic Mystery*. The collection of intimate poetry and short stories was well-received, garnering positive reviews on the popular book critic sites *Sistahs on the Shelf* and *RAW-SISTAZ Reviewers*.

Eternity continues her work in the writing realm as the founder of QueerBlackVoices, a visibility project dedicated to the collection of personal stories from out and proud Black queer-identified people. Eternity also aspires to start a literary services company devoted to supporting queer Black writers in making their work more accessible to the world.

K.A. Smith is a writer of poetry and fiction. Writing is her first love and women are her passion. She seamlessly merges the two to bring you sensual scenarios and titillating tales of women's love, sex, and desire. She's the author of *Get At Me, Gina's Do-Over,* and *The Players*. Her website is at krystalasmith.com. Follow her on Twitter @authorkasmith.

Ashley Sullivan is a Black lesbian femme who writes stories about Black women, for Black women. She lives and writes from the margins in small town America.

CPSIA information can be obtained
at www.ICGtesting.com
Printed in the USA
LVOW11s1107291017
554200LV00002B/459/P